# Dedication

*To the men and women of the
United States Armed Forces,
past, present, and future.*

# CONTENTS

*Chapter*

# INTRODUCTION

It was Thanksgiving Day, 1998. My mother's family had gathered for dinner at her house. After the meal, several of us, including my grandfather, sat and talked lazily while we waited for dessert. The conversation eventually turned to movies, and I mentioned that I had just seen *Saving Private Ryan*. Knowing little about my grandfather's service during the war, other than that he was wounded by a German grenade, I naively said, "Granddad, I bet you're glad you didn't have to go through what those guys did on D-Day." He quickly followed with, "How do you think I got to France? Omaha Beach, June 6, 1944."

To say there were a few stunned people at the table is an understatement. My mother's parents had nine children and none knew much about my grandfather's experiences during the war, much less that he landed on Omaha Beach on D-Day. He just didn't talk about it.

"You were there that day?"

"Yes son, I was."

We immediately threw a few questions at him, but his responses were short and measured. His window of conversation closed quickly, and soon the glimpse into that part of his past was gone.

In the months that followed I tried to pry a few stories out of him, feeling a bit like a trespasser on grounds that hadn't been crossed by anyone for a long, long time, if ever. From what little he offered, I learned he was a combat engineer during the invasion of France. He told me the story of Gen. George Patton giving him and the other troops a colorful, salty pep talk a few days before they crossed the English Channel. He mentioned that he had seen the Queen of England driving an ambulance while he was in London. Beyond those stories, I could tell it was something he was never comfortable discussing.

Robert Kenworthy, profiled in this book, said that asking a man to look into his past and share certain memories can be asking too much. Such is the case with my grandfather. When I asked him to share his story with me for this book he said, "Son, I lived it once and I don't want to live it again." End of conversation and understandably so. Who would fault someone for trying to forget an event marked by violence and death?

Regardless, he was there for the 20th century's most pivotal episode. It was a time that was revolting and violent, yet at the same time patriotic and inspirational. Its framing was set in black and white, without the tints of gray that have colored so many wars before and after. It plainly pitted the Allies against the Axis. Good guys, bad guys. As part of the fight for freedom and democracy, our country's purpose was clear, our actions deliberate. It has been called the "last good war," but I have learned that there was nothing good about it other than that it ended and we won.

On that Thanksgiving Day I learned that I had a deeper tie to our country's and world's history than I realized. Many of us do. We simply choose to not investigate it. Having that connection, I wanted to hear about the war through those who were there. For several months I had the honor of meeting and interviewing eighteen of Hampton Roads' World War II veterans. I did not search for those with the most heroic or tantalizing stories. That's not what I wanted. I simply interviewed those with whom I came in contact, or those I already knew.

Through their memories and emotions, I saw the colors of a war that I could only previously witness in black and white on the History Channel. After listening to their stories I decided that they needed to be heard by others. More importantly, remembered by others.

For the veterans themselves, many have tried to forget. For nearly fifty years they stuffed that part of their past away, hoping to suppress the violence and subdue the memories of the friends that were lost. But with the enormous press coverage that trumpeted the fiftieth anniversaries of D-Day and the end of the war, something changed. Realizing that time was erasing their living memories in our communities, they began to unlock the past by speaking and teaching. Their reasons are not for self-adulation. They simply don't want their sacrifices to be forgotten. They want the generations that follow to appreciate the freedoms and privileges they enjoy. As Neil Van Pelt, also in this book, puts it, "If we don't tell people about what we went through, who else will?"

Contrary to how the soldiers of World War II are sometimes portrayed, most were not martyrs for freedom. Were they the "Greatest Generation"? Maybe. Yet, the last place most of them wanted to be was in the military fighting a war. They were forced to leave their families and friends, not knowing if they would ever see them again. Many did not. Some 7,000 Virginians never came home. Yet a job was asked of them and without hesitation they did it. Even after the Great Depression had left a deep scar on millions of people, they volunteered. Even after many had lost hope not only in themselves, but in our country, they saluted the flag and marched off to war.

The war dominated daily life, especially here in Hampton Roads. As a major troop transport location, the streets of Norfolk were flooded by boys in uniform. Newport News Dry Dock and Shipbuilding quickly grew to 70,000 workers who toiled tirelessly as a part of the country's war machine. Locally, 428 vessels were manufactured and put into service. Machine gun nests were set up along the Virginia Beach oceanfront. German U-boats hunted within sight of our coast. Some still remain submerged off the Outer Banks. Nightly blackouts dimmed our neighborhoods. Even though the war was thousands of miles away, Hampton Roads was as close as you could get to the front lines at home.

Stars adorned windows on nearly every city street from the Eastern Shore to the Outer Banks. A blue star meant that family had someone in the service. A gold star meant they weren't coming back. Food ration books were distributed to limit how much of certain foods families could buy. Gas was rationed and non-essential driving was discouraged. Our communities rallied to collect scrap metal, rubber, and paper. Many families kept track of the war's progress on maps placed prominently in the home. And the list goes on. Our county was living a Norman Rockwell painting from coast to coast, at least on the surface.

The picture wasn't always rosy. Families left fatherless, a generation of young men lost to war, a segregated military, and the embarrassment of the Japanese internment camps were only a few of the home-front casualties.

There was no greater hatred in the world, other than that of the Russians for the Germans, than that felt by Americans for the Japanese. The Japanese sneak attack on Pearl Harbor struck a spinal nerve within the American public that brought it together in a singular, unified purpose: Make the Japanese pay for what they did. No longer were they Japanese, they were just Japs or Nips. While some may say this hatred was fueled in part by racist propaganda, many veterans I listened to say it was deserved. Some still feel that way. In this book, you will read several inflammatory comments that may be offensive to those of Japanese descent. Although I cannot speak for the veterans represented here, I simply ask that you remember the time frame from which their animosity stems.

The Germans on the other hand, were slightly, only slightly, a different story. Referred to as Krauts, Jerries, or Huns, they never quite pricked the spine of hate as the Japanese did. At least not in those with whom I've spoken. Was it because they were white and the Japanese weren't? Maybe, but I think it's deeper than that. Soldiers and the public alike seemed to view them differently than the Japanese. A comment I have heard time and time again is that the German soldiers were "respected" for their abilities as a fighting unit. As long as they weren't Nazis, according to those I interviewed, German soldiers typically weren't hated. Granted, our boys had no qualms in killing them, but it seems to have been more out of a need for survival than out of hate.

Regardless of which enemy we were fighting, World War II was a war that unleashed machines of death like the world had never seen. Guns, artillery, mines, planes, submarines, and bombs, two of which were atomic, all were designed and used to kill as many people as possible. Never in the history of man have so many people been killed by war: 26 million worldwide (13 million of these were Russian civilians), 34.4 million wounded. The toll at home was numbing: 403, 399 Americans killed, 671,846 wounded. When you consider the high cost of nearly 100,000 American lives between the two wars of Korea and Vietnam, you get some idea of the enormous price our families paid from 1941 to 1945.

Those numbers take on greater meaning when you actually sit down and listen to those who "kicked 'em in the Axis." Through them I have learned a great deal. These are lessons that will never come across on paper. They invited me into their homes and allowed me to ask them questions they avoided answering for decades. For some, it opened wounds that had been closed for a long time. For all, I believe, it was heartening that others wanted to hear their stories.

We are blessed in Hampton Roads to be enriched with the history that surrounds us. We are, of course, a military town. It's the life blood of our neighborhoods and our commerce. We are defined by it. You'll find our past alive in the gray-haired man sitting on the bench in the mall. It's in the elderly gentleman driving the car with the small American flag on the bumper. It's in the husband and wife next door who visit their friends' graves each Memorial Day at one of our local war memorials. Their presence around us truly is history next door.

But that living history is dying, literally. It has been estimated that more than 1,000 World War II veterans die each day. In 2001, most are between the ages of 75 and 85. They will not be with us much longer. The World War I generation has passed, and so too in short time will that of the second great war.

I have chosen to speak with our area's World War II veterans simply because I have a family tie to that generation. But their sacrifices and losses are no greater than that of those who served in our country's other wars and conflicts. You will hear the same sadness and pride from those who fought in Korea, Vietnam, the Gulf War, or any of our country's other conflicts. No group should be celebrated any more or any less than the other. All laid their lives on the line, and many gave the ultimate sacrifice. They gave their tomorrows for your today. For that, we owe them our respect and unending memory. I hope this book in some small way serves to do so.

1943

2000

S everal months before I met Bert Earnest, I had watched a National Geographic special on the Battle of Midway. Part of that special revolved around a torpedo bomber pilot and his radio man/tunnel gunner who had miraculously survived the devastating first hours of the battle. Of the six torpedo bombers that lifted off from Midway Island on the morning of June 4, 1942, only one plane returned, carrying the two pilots interviewed in the special.

When I met him at his Virginia Beach home, I only knew that Bert Earnest had been a pilot during the war. In fact, I was referred to him by his next door neighbor, Capt. John Reed, profiled later in this book. But as I looked at the memorabilia adorning the walls of his study, I noticed a painting of an American torpedo bomber squadron being attacked by Japanese fighters. At the bottom of the painting was an account of the frenetic scene stating that the only plane in the group to return to Midway Island that morning was piloted by Capt. Bert Earnest.

"Is that you?," I asked.

He nodded yes and simply said, "I got lucky that day."

Bert Earnest was born in Richmond with military in his blood. His father was a reserve officer in the Army, his uncle a regular in the Army, and his brother had attended Virginia Military Institute. Bert followed in their footsteps.

"I remember I went up to VMI for my brother's finals and I saw all these grown men, twenty-one-years old, crying when they were leaving, and that impressed the hell out of me. Plus, I sort of admired the life my uncle was living, and I liked the military way of life anyway."

By 1938 Earnest was commissioned as a second lieutenant in the field artillery reserve, and worked as a civil engineer for the next few years. He says it was obvious to him that America would be going to war eventually, so he expected to be called up soon with his Army artillery unit. He was right about the war, but not about being in the Army.

"The Army Air Corps came to Lexington and I decided it looked interesting. They gave us physicals and they found that my eyesight was great but I had a weak muscle in one eye, which I still have if I don't do my eye exercises. I would look straight ahead, but that one eye would look off to the right some. They said I could walk down the street and look at girls on both sides of the street. Well, that wasn't quite so, but it did make it so I couldn't join the Air Corps.

"Then the Navy came through Richmond, and they came over town in a dive bomber and put it in a low pitch and made all the noise in the world. So everybody ran out to the airfield to see the Navy plane. A friend of mine decided he wanted to take the Navy physical, but I didn't go because I knew I had the eye problem. Well, the next day he had to go back, and I went along with him. I ended up taking the physical and they found the same problem but said it was very easy to fix with eye exercises and that I could have it fixed in no time!

"So I did the eye exercises and a month later I retook the test and passed it. And then there I was thinking, 'Ok, you have a reserve commission in the Army. So do you go in the Navy as a seaman second class? What are you going to do?' I thought about it a while and decided that the Navy had been pretty good to me so I went with the Navy. But it might have had something to do with some movie I had seen that had fighter planes flying off a carrier. It looked pretty glamorous."

After giving up his commission as an Army officer, Earnest was sent to naval flight training at Anacostia Airfield, outside of Washington, D.C. The new recruits were put through four weeks of "elimination training." Those that were able to complete a solo flight at the end of the four weeks graduated to advanced training. Those that failed were washed out of the training. Earnest passed.

"After basic and instrument training in Jacksonville, we had to decide if we wanted to go through carrier aviation, patrol aviation, or train for the aircraft that flew off battleships and cruisers. So I picked carrier, which meant I had to go down to Miami. We flew dive bombers and fighters, but the only thing we didn't fly were torpedo bombers. Well, then my orders came in and they had assigned me to a torpedo squadron!"

There were three main types of attack aircraft in 1941: fighters, scout (dive) bombers, and torpedo bombers. Fighters were fast, had guns in the wings, and were the ones that everybody wanted to fly. The dive bombers were heavier and not as maneuverable, but were good planes. The torpedo plane was the biggest, heaviest, and slowest of the three because it had to carry a 2,000-pound torpedo in its belly.

"I knew the job of a torpedo pilot was risky business. The point of the torpedo bomber was that if you could get at a ship with a torpedo, you would be hitting beneath the water and then you had a pretty good chance of sinking it. But it was risky because you had to get down close to do it." The pilots were to penetrate the screen of enemy fighters and ships, stay low and slow, and drop a torpedo at an enemy vessel. "It didn't seem like a recipe for a long life." For many, it wasn't.

Earnest was sent to Norfolk to join Torpedo Squadron 8 (VT-8), assigned to the newly christened aircraft carrier *Hornet*. "I was in the latest and newest of the air groups, but I was in an airplane I didn't particularly want to fly."

By November, 1941, he had finished flight training and was able to take leave in Richmond. While he was there the Japanese pilots ravaged Pearl Harbor. "After the attack, I checked with the Navy folks in Richmond to see if they needed me immediately. They told me I wasn't due back until December 10 and that they thought they could do without me for three days.

"When my leave was up I remember being pretty worried while driving into Norfolk. I was listening to the radio and heard about two British ships that had been sunk off Singapore. That didn't sound very good, but I had the job."

As Earnest returned to Norfolk, *Hornet* was on her shakedown cruise and was too busy to give new pilots, like Earnest, further training for carrier aviation. Although their general training was completed, new pilots still needed to acquire a certain number of flying hours to be carrier-qualified. So with their ship at sea, the plebe pilots did their training over land instead of water.

"We flew like mad in Norfolk for about a month trying to get flying time in after the *Hornet* and VT-8 returned. Landing on a carrier is just a technique you learn. Theoretically the landing was pretty simple, but it could get a little rough depending on the breezes and so forth. You practice on the field a lot before you go at it, and we'd spend all day out there doing field-carrier landing practice. My log book shows five flights in one day. The C.O. said that if we weren't flying he wanted us in one of the other seats, which we didn't appreciate at all. He said any time in the air was good time. So we'd go up in the air with the other guys and they'd scare us to death, then we'd scare them to death."

VT-8, Earnest's squadron, had been chosen to receive the first of the new Grumman TBF-1s, a new torpedo bomber that was far superior to what they had been flying. But the new planes wouldn't be ready before *Hornet* set sail for the Pacific. So, half the squadron, including Earnest, was left behind to receive the new planes.

By early May, 1942, VT-8 had received 21 of their new TBF-1s. "Grumman hadn't even finished testing them. They weren't sure how fast they could go in a dive, and we got them up to about 350 knots and the wing fillets started pulling loose, so we decided that was too fast. It turned out later they put the restriction at 315 knots. It was a fast, superior aircraft compared to what we had been flying. They were about as fast as the fighters were at the time. But later in the war they kept adding more and more equipment which made them slower and slower.

"The Grumman people came down to put in the fixes they didn't have time to put in at the factory. One of those things was bulletproof fuel tanks which I was very, very thankful for later. They also put armored plating behind the pilot's seat, which I was also thankful for because at Midway I would hear the bullets rattling ting-ting-ting off that plating."

While the final modifications were being made to the new planes in Norfolk, *Hornet* was on the West Coast receiving a group of B-25 bombers that would soon make headlines across the world. This group would be the first bombers to strike at the heart of Japan by flying a bombing raid over Tokyo. Called the Doolittle Raid after it's commander, Jimmy Doolittle, the raid inflicted little damage, yet completed its two-pronged mission: to boost American morale, and to prove to the Japanese that they weren't invincible.

As *Hornet* moved farther into the Pacific, Earnest and the rest of the torpedo pilots still in Norfolk were issued orders to join the squadron immediately. "We didn't know it, but Midway was coming up. The commanders probably knew it, but we didn't."

The island of Midway is a speck of volcanic outcropping in the middle of the Pacific Ocean. More than 1,000 miles from Hawaii, 3,000 from Japan, it was a crucial U.S. base early in the war. Though small in size, it would be the center of one of the war's greatest naval battles. It was at Midway that the tide of the war in the Pacific would turn.

The Americans and Japanese had just finished slugging it out in the Battle of the Coral Sea. Although considered a draw, the battle did not go well for the Americans. The carrier *Lexington* was sunk and *Yorktown* was badly damaged.

With the U.S. Navy weakened, the Japanese saw an opportunity for a decisive, fatal blow that would give them domination of the Pacific. If they could decimate and take the American garrison at Midway, the Americans would be left only with Pearl Harbor.

The Imperial Japanese Navy planned its surprise attack on Midway for early June, 1942. Not taking any chances, the Japanese mustered the full might of their fleet against the tiny U.S. force at Midway. But American code breakers had already learned of the Japanese plot. Having uncovered a priceless jewel of information, the U.S. fleet began preparing for a risky ambush.

The Japanese were convinced that the American carriers would be in Pearl Harbor, leaving Midway unguarded by any significant force. But in a miracle of ingenuity and sweat, workers at Pearl Harbor had pieced together the wounded *Yorktown* in only three days (the Navy was initially told it would take 12 weeks for repairs), giving the Americans three carriers with which to attack. Arriving just north of Midway, they waited for the massive Japanese fleet.

While the Americans scrambled to meet the oncoming Japanese forces, Bert Earnest was just arriving in Pearl Harbor. It was almost six months after the attack there. "It still looked like hell. There was oily water everywhere. It was a mess."

Armed with the new TBF-1s planes, Earnest and the small detachment of torpedo bombers had arrived one day after their ship *Hornet* had set out for the battle. Yet instead of sending all the new planes to *Hornet*, naval commanders decided to send six of them to Midway to bolster defenses of the island. "I volunteered like all the rest of them did. We didn't know what we were going to do, we just knew it was something different. But we'd get in the war and that's what we came out there for." Along with 17 other young, eager, yet inexperienced pilots, Bert Earnest was selected to go to Midway.

On June 1 the detachment of six torpedo bombers took off from Pearl Harbor and headed for Midway. "It was an eight-hour flight and was the first time I had flown out of sight of land in my life." The crews joined Navy, Army, and Marine flight crews already there. By then the island was heavily defended with artillery, antiaircraft guns, and hundreds of men.

Earnest's superiors were blunt with him and the other pilots. A Japanese attack was imminent. The odds were not good. If one of their torpedo planes could get through, they would consider the attack a success. Earnest's previous notion that being a torpedo bomber pilot was "not a recipe for long life" seemed dead right.

The plan was for patrol planes to go out and search for the Japanese fleet. When the fleet was found, all aircraft at Midway would attack. Fighters would defend the island against enemy planes, bombers would strike the ships.

On June 2 the pilots prepared for their first combat mission. "We got up at about 4:00 A.M. to man the airplanes, start the engines, and sit in the cockpit. Then we got the all clear, we cut the engines, and got out. We then spent the day checking out our equipment, wandering around the island, or chasing gooney birds."

June 3 was the same. A few moments of early morning anxiety, then long hours of waiting for the rest of the day. "The fighter pilots had a hut right alongside the runway and I had a bunk in one of them. I was walking down the runway to go to bed on the 3rd, and I found a two-dollar bill laying on the ground. I picked it up and put it in my billfold. I've never flown without that two-dollar bill."

June 4 started like the previous two mornings, but the monotony was soon broken. "A Marine officer rode up in a jeep and climbed up on the wing of the flight leader and told him something. Then someone came up to me and said, 'Enemy ships at 320 degrees, 150 miles!' I don't deny being scared. It didn't scare me enough, though. I got scared later when the bullets were flying around and hitting the wings. But that doesn't stop you from doing what you intend to do."

On board with Earnest was his radioman and tunnel gunner, Harry Ferrier, and his turret gunner, Jay Manning. Both men were only about 18 years old. Earnest was the old man of the crew at age 25. As Ferrier would later say, "We were only teenagers, so we thought we were immortal. We thought we had the best planes in the Navy and that we were going to give the Japanese hell, and come back. It didn't work out that way."

Earnest recalls, "The fighters were already taking off and we were right behind them. We had just been in the air a couple of minutes and my turret gunner said he could see firing back at the island. The Japanese aircraft had gotten there right after we had all just gotten off the ground. They came down strafing the field so they would have gotten any airplanes down there.

"Then just about that time two planes made a run at us and passed us by. Our squadron commander tried to get some spirit into us by giving us a big fist, which was the squadron's symbol for attack. We decided to show our motto for "invade"." Earnest then shows how the pilots displayed their middle finger to one another. "That was our little signal to each other in the air.

"We must have flown about an hour, and I thought I saw a ship ahead of us. Looked like a transport to me. At that time Manning called and said we were being attacked by fighters. Then I looked back down at the water and there was the whole Japanese fleet ahead of me. We had found them right dead on the nose. I could see two carriers that were well ahead of us.

"We opened our bombay doors. We knew all along that if you didn't open them and the hydraulic system was shot out, then you couldn't drop the torpedo. We dove on down to our approach altitude of 200 feet. Japanese fighters were making runs on us all the way. They were all around us, so many that they seemed to be getting in each other's way. There must have been 25 of them. The Zero fighter was the most maneuverable aircraft I had ever seen. Manning fired the turret gun a number of times, but soon it fell silent.

"Ferrier looked up to see why and saw Manning hanging limp in the safety harness, obviously dead, but I didn't know that at the time." Ferrier recalled later, "Quite suddenly I was a scared, mature old man at the age of 18." Ferrier tried to fire his own gun but the hydraulic system had been shot out and the tail wheel had dropped down, blocking his firing lane.

"The fighters were behind us, but I just happened to see one pass in front of me and tried to take a shot at it. But when I tried to fire my one .30-cal gun, it wouldn't fire. "Then I had some 20mm cannon shells hitting out at the wings. You talk about being scared. That's when I really got scared. They were just huge explosions. Well, a piece of shrapnel came through the canopy and hit me in the cheek and blood just went all over the place. And about that time my elevator control went dead. We were only at a couple of hundred feet anyway, and with my elevator gone, I thought, 'Man, that's it. I'm going in the water.'

By this time the formation of six planes was in shambles. About halfway to the carriers the planes were forced to break formation, which they weren't supposed to do. Also, Earnest had now lost contact with both Ferrier and Manning, assuming both men were dead. With his crew down to one, and his airplane steadily dropping toward the sea, he tried for a last ditch effort to strike at one of the Japanese ships.

"I wanted to get rid of the torpedo, and there was a Japanese ship off to port. So with the rudder and aileron I was able to get a lead on the ship and try to drop the torpedo before I hit the water. I dropped the torpedo (it didn't hit), but I felt horrible about leaving the formation because you just don't do that. I had to, though. I more or less stood by to hit the water because there wasn't anything I could do. I was within seconds of being dead.

"Right when I was about to hit the water I rolled the trim tab, which I always did in a normal landing (the trim tab helps the plane fly level). When I did that the airplane jumped up in the air and I realized I could fly it with the trim tab. But two Japanese fighters decided they didn't want me flying anymore.

"They came after me. They chased me for what seemed like five hours, but I doubt if it was five minutes. They kept making runs at me, but there wasn't anything I could do since they were faster than me. I'd turn and try to evade them but I couldn't. All of a sudden there was dead silence. No more machine guns firing. No more bullets hitting the armor plating right behind my head. So I looked around and they were gone. I don't know to this day why they left, whether they ran out of ammunition, or were getting too far from their ship, or were called back because more planes were coming in."

The planes that were coming in were more torpedo bombers and dive bombers from the U.S. aircraft carriers *Hornet*, *Enterprise* and *Yorktown*. Their results were dismally similar to that of Earnest's, yet on a much bigger scale. As the American pilots made their approaches on the Japanese ships, they were blown out of the sky. Losses were appalling. *Enterprise* lost 18 of 28 pilots. *Yorktown* lost 21 of 24 pilots. And on Earnest's ship, *Hornet*, only one of 31 pilots survived. After all those losses, not one torpedo had found its mark.

Bert Earnest was oblivious to all of this as he struggled to get his battered aircraft back to Midway. He repeatedly called his crew members but there was no answer. "Then about fifteen minutes later, Ferrier called me. He had just come to. He had been grazed by a bullet in the head that went right through his baseball cap and simply knocked him out. It didn't injure him badly at all. Manning, he told me, was dead."

Although Earnest had survived the Japanese fighters, his turning and twisting from trying to evade them had put the Japanese fleet directly between him and Midway. "I looked back at the Japanese fleet and I couldn't see any damage to any ships. I didn't know where the rest of my people were. So I climbed up to a couple thousand feet. I checked my compass, but it was shot out. But the sun was still rising in the east, so I used that to navigate.

"I decided I wasn't about to go back over their fleet, but that was in the direction of Midway. So I thought I'd fly south until I got opposite of Midway, then I would turn east toward the island until I found it. It was just guess work. Eventually I saw this big plume of black smoke so I thought I'd go down to see what it was, and on my way down I saw this island called Kure Island which I knew was fifty miles west of Midway. So I knew I was going to get home because I could make it fifty miles.

"When I got back to Midway I made my recognition turn and tried to put the landing gear down and only one gear would come down. So I went up and shook the airplane a little bit, but nothing happened. So I came in to make my approach and there was a Marine out there waving me off. I took the wave off and was thinking maybe the torpedo was still in the bombay. I asked Ferrier, 'Can you see whether the torpedo is gone?' There was a viewing window right underneath the turret, but Manning was bleeding all over it so Ferrier couldn't see. So we didn't know if it was gone or not.

"We came in for another landing, got another wave off, and I decided, 'Hell with it, I'm going to land this plane.' Apparently they were trying to call me on the radio to tell me to go out and bail out. Well I wouldn't have done that anyway. I had a wounded crewman and a dead crewman, and I was wounded. They didn't want me to block the runway but that wasn't my worry at the time. I just wanted to get on the ground.

"I landed very nicely. The plane rolled down the runway and finally lost lift on the right wing and spun around and parked right off the runway like it was before." Crews would find that the aircraft had been hit by 64 machine gun bullets and nine 20mm cannon shells. Of the two Navy Crosses Earnest was awarded for the Battle of Midway, one was for simply being able to get his airplane back safely. The other was awarded for flying the mission.

Bert Earnest and Harry Ferrier waited for the other planes in their detachment to return. "We waited around for a long time, but nobody came back. Yeah, I expected them to come back, but they didn't. The Japs shot them all down."

Through the early morning hours of June 4, the Americans were losing the battle. In a last ditch effort, it was decided to launch all available planes from the carriers in hopes of catching the Japanese aircraft while they were being refueled on the flight decks. It was there that they would be most vulnerable. It was a gamble that would pay dividends for the rest of the war.

American dive bombers lifted off in search of the four Japanese carriers. When they found them, they indeed found their decks packed with planes and fuel containers. And more importantly, there were no fighters in the air to protect them. The bombers attacked, and within just five minutes three of the carriers were ablaze and headed to the bottom of the Pacific Ocean. It was a devastating loss from which the Japanese would never recover.

With the battle over, Earnest was sent back to Pearl Harbor and placed in another torpedo squadron. In just a few short months he would find himself on an airfield in a place called Guadalcanal. Assigned to the carrier *Saratoga*, Earnest's squadron was deployed to attack the large Japanese naval force that had cut off the Marines already on the island. That large Japanese force eventually took aim on *Saratoga*, sinking her. With no carrier on which to land, Earnest was forced to fly his missions, when possible, from the newly won Henderson Field on Guadalcanal.

Earnest says one of the longest nights of his life was spent there. "They came in and hit us with battleships and everything else. They wrecked all of our airplanes, then we had nothing to do but hide! Our tents were in a coconut grove very close to the airfield, but we had to get out of them. I got into a half-dug fox hole where I had to fight a rat for space. That was a pretty bad time. To be shelled by battleships, that's not what you expect when you sign up for an aviation squadron on a carrier. Plus, we nearly got captured there. It was tight there for a while."

Fortunately, more Marines with more aircraft were beginning to resupply the beleaguered Americans. With more planes at hand, Earnest and the other pilots were called upon almost daily to contend with the Japanese ships still harassing the island. "I made four torpedo attacks from Guadalcanal. One from *Saratoga*, the others from the island. I only saw one torpedo hit. I used to tell people who would ask if I hit anything, 'Man, I don't know. I was running in the other direction!' But I did see one hit." He was awarded a Japanese sword for that hit.

After two long months at Guadalcanal, Bert Earnest finally had the chance to get back home. He says he spent a year "not doing much of anything." But by late 1943 he was called upon again and was sent back to the Pacific. "I wanted to go back in a fighter that time, but they said, 'Are you kidding? You're an experienced torpedo pilot!'"

Looking back he says he had a small feeling as he returned to action that his luck was running out. Not only did his luck not run out, he was awarded his third Navy Cross during the Battle of the Eastern Solomons. "I got that one for receiving credit for sinking a Japanese ship, but I still think it was the dive bombers that may have gotten them."

By July 1944, Capt. Bert Earnest was home for good. He would spend the next 28 years in the Navy, part of that time as a test pilot. In 1990 he was inducted into the Carrier Aviation Hall of Fame on board the new *U.S.S. Yorktown*.

Bert Earnest is the last torpedo pilot still living from the Battle of Midway. Because of his miraculous survival, he is frequently asked to recount his harrowing mission. It's an incredible story that he's happy to share, but he keeps it framed in the reality of lives lost. "I don't have any guilt about my survival, but I'm just so sorry that so many others didn't. The good Lord wasn't ready to take me at that time, that was all."

1943                                         2000

He was beaten mercilessly with a sword by the first Japanese soldier he saw. It was his beginning to a hellish three and a half years. His fear, suffering, and determination can only be understood by those who shared his plight. His captors were inhumane and murderous. Their acts of atrocities continue to reach beyond the scope of understanding, and for many, forgiveness.

Bob Simmons grew up as a country boy in Columbus County, N.C. His father was able to buy a farm there, which allowed him to provide for his wife and six children. The way Simmons looks at it, his family was one of the lucky ones during the lean times of the 1930s. "We had plenty to eat and plenty of clothes, but that was about it," smiles Simmons.

But as he grew into his late teens, Simmons realized that work outside of the farm was hard to find. Bread lines outnumbered paychecks in rural North Carolina during the Depression. So, like thousands of other young men across the country, he joined the military, partly because of the adventure, but mainly because it was a job with steady pay.

In 1940 his reason for joining the Navy was simple. "It sounded like an awful lot of walking in the Army." He was immediately sent to Norfolk for recruit training, and then applied for and was accepted to submarine school in New Haven, Conn. "We got to choose where we wanted to go, and I wanted to go out to Hawaii. I went and I liked it, but the next thing I knew they were changing our home port to Cavite in the Philippine Islands!"

Simmons was sent across the Pacific to Manila on the submarine *U.S.S Shark*. Manila may have been halfway around the world from his Carolina farm, but for the most part being stationed in the Philippines was a good hitch at that time. Americans were treated well, the islands were beautiful, and it seemed to be a safe, cozy place to serve out your time in the service. Even though war with Japan seemed inevitable to those in Washington, it didn't to Simmons or his fellow crew. "We just didn't think Japan would do that."

In fact, on their way to Pearl Harbor the Japanese had sneaked by Simmons' patrol. The Japanese attack left the remainder of American forces in the Pacific Rim and Asia without a sustainable defense. The very next day the first Japanese planes attacked the Philippines, destroying most of the planes while they were still on the ground. Gen. Douglas MacArthur's unwinnable defense of the Philippine Islands had begun.

Shortly after the Japanese invasion of the Philippines started, Simmons had a life-saving transfer. "One day, some chief came over to me and said, "Hey Simmons, come here. Do you see that ship out there?' It was a sea-going yacht. It was pretty. He said, 'How would you like to be on that?' I told him I'd like that!" Simmons was told that if he and some other men could get it running they would be transferred to it from their submarine, *Shark*. Simmons had been trained to work on the diesel engines of that time and had it running that day. They then gave the ship a Navy christening, giving her the name *Mary Anne*. She was outfitted with torpedoes and a .50 caliber machine gun and assigned to inner-island patrol. The crew's job was to cruise the islands looking for Japanese trying to invade behind American lines.

The transfer saved his life. Two months after the *Shark* left the Philippines for patrol somewhere in the South China Sea, she and her crew of 58 men were never heard from again. Sunk by the Japanese in February, 1942, the *Shark* was one of the first U.S. submarines lost in World War II. "If I had stayed on there, I would've been blown up."

During the early part of 1942 the Japanese continued their brutal advance across the Philippines, closing in on the American strongholds. Gen. MacArthur ordered all American and Filipino forces to withdraw to the Bataan Peninsula, while he, his staff, non-combatants, and a small number of Marines and Army personnel retreated to the small island of Corregidor. Corregidor, or "the Rock," was just offshore from Bataan and was to serve as headquarters until the make-believe American Fleet could come to the rescue. That rescue would never come, despite MacArthur's promises that it would. The only thing that came were more Japanese. By March 1942 the Fil-American forces at Bataan were decimated by casualties, disease, lack of medical supplies, and food. Their situation was desperate, and turning hopeless.

Meanwhile, Simmons and the crew of the *Mary Anne* continued their search for Japanese trying to sneak behind American lines at Bataan. They spent their days circling Corregidor, then moved over to Bataan at night. "One early morning the Marines contacted us and told us they thought the Japanese had landed behind them, so they wanted us to go try to find out where they were. There were a lot of caves and beaches and a lot of good places to land. So we went into this one place we thought they might be. We strafed the beaches with the .50 caliber and we didn't see a thing. So went in again, got closer, and strafed the beaches again. Nothing. The next time, they told us we'd be able to see the whites of their eyes if they were in there. So we went in, and they opened up on us. And let me tell you, they had a lot of people in there! They had rifles, artillery, mortars. When we'd turn, I'd jump on the other side of the sandbags. That was our armor. I don't know how in the world I kept from getting hit. It was just like a swarm of bees coming over your head. We finally got out of there and told the Marines where they were, and the Marines got 'em.

"Another night, we ran up on a Japanese vessel. We didn't dare shoot at it because we didn't have anything to hurt it. It seemed like the biggest ship I had ever seen. We were trying to get out of there, so I had to put the engines in reverse. But the engines were so hot I couldn't get 'em in reverse. I finally did it, but that was a scary, scary moment. I can tell it with humor now, but I couldn't then. Oh my goodness."

Simmons' crew soon became known as "Captain Knowles and his 21 Thieves." Since any type of supplies had become a high commodity on Bataan and Corregidor, the crew of the *Mary Anne* boarded destroyed ships, American or Japanese, looking for whatever they could use. But any finds they made were only a drop in the bucket of decay that had befallen the U.S. forces.

By early March MacArthur was ordered to evacuate to Australia. Simmons said MacArthur's departure was one of the few things he did that the men were happy about. "We didn't like MacArthur. We were hungry before we were ever captured because he would say that a soldier fought better on an empty stomach. We would say to ourselves, 'Why are you doing this? The Japanese are going to get this place and all the food anyhow.'"

By early April the food at Bataan had run out, and the Fil-American forces were only fighting at 30 percent of their strength due to malnutrition, disease, casualties and pure exhaustion. On April 9, 76,000 men were surrendered at Bataan, beginning one of the most appalling events of the war, the Bataan Death March.

Much has been written of the deplorable treatment of Allied prisoners by their Japanese captors. Yet rarely is it accompanied by how the Japanese viewed surrender. Many of those in the Japanese military were instructed in a code of conduct in which surrender was unthinkable. It showed cowardice that disgraced not only the soldier, but also his homeland and the Emperor. Suicide was expected before surrender. Conversely, to die in battle was the greatest honor. Working from this mindset, the Japanese felt well within their rights to treat their prisoners as subhuman. Also important to note is that the Japanese government never ratified its agreement to the Geneva Convention Relative to the Treatment of Prisoners. Bob Simmons would learn the consequences of this firsthand.

When Bataan fell, the Japanese then focused their might on the last remaining bastion of American strength, Corregidor. Simmons and the crew of the *Mary Anne* continued to make their patrols around the island, yet had decided that if Corregidor was to be surrendered as well, they were going to make a run for it to Australia. They would never get that chance.

One night Simmons could hear the mass of Japanese assault boats coming across the water to Corregidor. As the enemy approached the beaches, the U.S. troops on the island, and the *Mary Anne*, fired into them, killing many. "But they just kept coming. There wasn't an end to them. It was like a tree shedding leaves on a stream, that's how all those Japanese looked floating in the water.

"We went in the next morning because they told us to go in and get some rest in the caves in Corregidor. When we pulled up, by George, they had already surrendered! The Japanese came down to the pier where we tied up. The first Japanese I saw beat the tar out of me with his hands and a sword. I thought he was going to cut my head off. I was a scared little boy."

After being detained in the man-made tunnels for a few days, Simmons and the other American and Filipino prisoners were marched to a nearby garage area that had been used for housing planes. Some 12,000 POWs were crammed into the facility, given small amounts of rice twice a day, then assigned numbers. After two weeks there, Japanese transport steamers arrived to ferry the prisoners to Manila. From there they would be sent to prison camps.

There were only three transport steamers and 12,000 POWs. That meant approximately 4,000 people were crammed into each ship. No toilets were made available, no water was given. The trip took only half a day, but the stench, heat and overcrowding made for a miserable voyage.

Once in Manila, the prisoners of Corregidor, including Simmons, embarked on their own march. "That's where we started our trip to the prison camp. That was long. I don't know how I made it. Luckily, I was in pretty good shape. But water is something that is hard to do without. Men would try to suck water out of the mud. They would shoot you for that. They didn't care who they shot, they just wanted others to see what would happen to them if they tried to stop."

The captives were marched through the streets of Manila for public display. Risking beatings or death, some Filipinos defied the Japanese and tried to sneak over to the prisoners to give them water and food. The Filipino sympathy for the Americans baffled the Japanese. They could not understand why the Filipinos would be more eager to help the white man, rather than someone closer to their own nationality. Obviously, the Filipinos were keen enough to realize who would treat them better. Soon after their parade through Manila, the POWs were stuffed into Bilibid Prison. Simmons says that his short stay there was quiet, and compared to what was to come, pleasant. There were toilets and showers, and a meal of thin rice soup was served three times a day. But the prison was severely overcrowded, which meant another move and another sad chapter in his plight.

Simmons and the other prisoners were then marched back to Manila to board trains that would take them to prison camps near the town of Cabanatuan. He and the others were packed into boxcars like chickens packed into crates on their way to the slaughterhouse. There was no room to sit on most of the cars, and the heat became overwhelming. There was no water. A few of the sick and wounded died while standing, supported only by the sheer number of men pressing in against them. When the men arrived in Cabanatuan that evening, they were forced to walk another five miles to one of the three prison camps awaiting them.

"When I got there, I thought I could not take another step," Simmons says slowly. He was sent to Camp Three. "There were all kinds of sicknesses and diseases and malnutrition. You couldn't get up at night without stepping on someone that was dead."

The only relief Simmons received at Camp Three was a slight break in the brutality from the guards. "I don't know if they had mellowed a bit, or had just done so much to so many people, but they let up on us a little bit. But they were still mean. They would shoot people, and beat them, and bayonet them. And then there were so many dead that they took us from Camp Three to Camp One."

Also in Cabanatuan were some of the survivors from Bataan. Those from Bataan had only been POWs a month longer, but their physical conditions and appearances were noticeably worse than those coming from Corregidor. In their first nine months at Cabanatuan approximately 3,000 Americans would die, mostly those who were surrendered in Bataan.

Cabanatuan was a dismal, dirty place. Simmons doesn't recall many specifics of his time there, but others do. Allen Laurence was a member of the Texas National Guard who had survived the fighting in Bataan and the Death March. He was eventually transferred to the same camp as Simmons. I came across his published journal on the internet, which described everyday life at Cabanatuan as this:

"We were assigned to a specific barrack, and then into groups of 10 for accountability, security, and work assignments. We were told that if one escaped, the other nine in the group would be shot. Those physically able were assigned for work on the farm, or duty on the ranch area (they kept about 50-100 head of Brahman cattle for meat; we never got any however), or to burial detail, or to wood detail which we liked *because it gave us a chance to get some mangoes or other food. I was on several burial details which buried 10 to 20 bodies in mass graves; most of the time the hole was filled with water so the bodies had to be held down so that soil could be thrown over the bodies. Earlier details buried 100 or more bodies at times. The death rate slowed down about November 1942...Insofar as I know there was no medicine for use by medical personnel. We had no toothbrushes or razors; we used grass, or anything else after defecating (those with bad diarrhea used nothing in most cases). Bedbugs lived by the thousands on the bamboo slats of the sleeping platform and ate on us at night. One's hand would be covered with blood after rubbing his body and/or the bamboo sleeping platform at night. To kill them we took the platforms out in the sunlight which killed them, we mashed those remaining if we could find them. Of course, we had no way to kill the eggs which were in the grass or bamboo ties. Our diet consisted of boiled rice and greens most of the time. Occasionally, we would get a little dried, wormy fish or soybean curd for our soup. We got half of a Red Cross package about Christmas of 1942 and a whole one another time before I left in September of 1943. I can't recall any clothing being distributed while I was in Cabanatuan; I wore what I came with."*

That's what life was like for almost one year of Bob Simmons' life.

One of the main vegetables grown at Cabanatuan was eggplant. It was only for the Japanese, yet Simmons says he wouldn't have eaten it even if they had offered it to him. "They'd dip stuff out of the toilets and fill up these two buckets and hang them on a pole, then carry it out there and pour it on those eggplants. They didn't throw that human waste away. They'd grow the biggest, prettiest eggplants you ever saw. We didn't eat them. Of course, they didn't want to share them with us, but we still didn't want to eat them."

After his time in Cabanatuan, Simmons and thousands of other POWs were then dispersed to various other camps in the Philippines, China, Japan, and Korea, where they were used as slave labor. Those who left the Philippines were transported on cargo ships which came to be known as "Hell Ships." "We went on a cattle ship. They had cleaned it out, but not for us," recalls Simmons. These ships were often packed tightly with prisoners in the stagnant, cramped bowels below decks. Simmons doesn't remember receiving much food on his trip, yet vaguely recalls that pots were passed around for the POWs. Toilets were typically kettles that had been placed in the middle of the cargo area. Once again, lack of water, food, medical treatment, and fresh air took their toll on the prisoners. Adding to the tragedy of these Hell Ships was the Japanese refusal to mark them as POW ships, which meant they were targets for American planes and submarines. Thousands of American POWs died at sea during their transport as a result of these attacks.

After the long journey north, Simmons was sent to a prison camp in Niigata, Japan, to work as a slave laborer, something strictly prohibited by the Geneva Convention. Niigata was a seaport on the main island of Honshu, just

16

north of Tokyo. There were several prison camps there, detaining thousands of Allied POWs. Simmons says one of the big shocks to him was the change in climate. "Oh, I'll tell you, that was cold. I was really surprised at that." Prisoners were issued Japanese winter clothing that included an overcoat and a grass raincoat, shoes and a couple of blankets. Body lice continued to be a problem, infesting clothes and bedding.

Conditions were still deplorable, but Simmons says that the death rate leveled once they were in Japan. "We didn't die wholesale like we did in the Philippines, but we didn't get as much to eat either. The rice and vegetables we had received in the Philippines were not given to us at Niigata. What we would get to eat would be boiled barley for breakfast. That stuff was just like rubber. The midday meal was the roots from an Australian radish. For the evening meal we'd get the tops of the radish." Simmons says that despite the monotony, he never tired of eating the same thing every day. Regardless of what it was, it was food.

"That was miserable living. That's what you call starving to death." To avoid actually doing so, some prisoners would supplement their diets by scrounging for and eating worms and rats. "I felt that desperate, but I never ate those things."

In an attempt to keep the prisoners fed and their spirits up, the Red Cross sent packages to them. The boxes were approximately a square foot in size, yet the prisoners received only a scraping of its contents due to the looting by Japanese guards. Not until the last few months of the war did prisoners receive them on a regular basis. During the years preceding that, though, Japanese guards fed themselves on the chocolates and canned meats in those Red Cross packages.

Simmons recounts the story of a group of prisoners emboldened enough by hunger to sneak out of camp at night through a sewer pipe that took them to the other side of the bamboo fence. They would then work their way over to a set of railroad tracks where boxcars containing food and supplies would sit idle at times. The men were lucky enough not to get caught, and were also able to steal quite a prize of soybeans.

"When they brought them back we would pull our rice straw mats back and pour the soybeans under the straw so that when the guards came to look for it they wouldn't see it. Those prisoners had to quit doing it because the Japanese were causing such a fuss over it. We knew we were going to get caught. If someone got caught stealing something, which was food usually, they'd find out which hand he stole it with and break the bones in that arm. They'd take the butt of a gun and wham! After that we wouldn't see them anymore. They'd send them off to another part of the camp."

The persistent abuse of the Allied POWs by the Japanese military was repulsive. "They were awful people," Simmons states sternly. But he quickly follows by saying that was their training, and there was quite a bit of physical violence not only within the Japanese ranks, but also towards the Japanese civilians. But make no mistake, their full abuse was directed at the Allied POWs.

Simmons says the main tactic by the prisoners was simply to try to stay away from their captors as much as they could. But complete avoidance was impossible. "An officer came up to me one day in the bunkhouse and yelled at me as loud as he could, 'Yoski!' That meant 'Attention!'. So I went to attention as fast as he wanted me to. But he whipped his sword around and hit me with it right across the neck. I was in front of a bunk, so that helped me to keep standing. It hurt but I didn't get to see my head roll. I was praying that lightning would strike him dead."

Any verbal response from a prisoner that could be viewed in any way as disrespectful brought punishment. "They would beat the tar out of you for that. You can just take so much of it and then you snap. But if you did say something, you wouldn't do it again the next day." Simmons squints as he recalls how painful the butt of a gun against the head is. "Now that my hair keeps falling out you can probably see some scars up there."

Simmons recalls a "pep talk" one of the officers delivered to the prisoners one morning. "He made a speech one day and made sure we all heard it. He said the Japanese were smarter than we were and that they were going to whip the United States, and that all Americans would be prisoners and that we ought to work or else."

Simmons was assigned to a steel mill in Niigata, working primarily with the blast furnaces. "Those things were hot. In the winter time it felt good. But they pulled us out of there in the winter and put Japanese in there. They'd then put us on the details that were outside.

"Before sunrise we were on our way and we didn't get home until after dark. I say home, but I mean where they kept us. And, oh man, why they put us so far from that factory I don't know. That's why we had to get up so early and go back after dark. They didn't put us on any truck. The only ride I had was on the train from Manila, and it didn't even go all the way."

Despite their shared plight, there were occasional riffs between the prisoners. "There was a fellow they put me to work with, and I don't know why they put me with him," Simmons says as he shakes his head. "But he was getting ready to get us both flogged. He was about to do something to get us in trouble, but I don't remember exactly what it was. I said, 'Hey man, you're going to get us killed.' And he gave me some kind of smart answer and asked me if I wanted to do something about it. I said yeah, because we were all a bit on the edge all the time. So we went outside so none of the Japanese would see us. After we got through with it and I thought it was all over, he dusted himself off and so did I. And all of a sudden all I could see were stars. That guy had taken a yoho pole and hit me over the head with all the strength he had. He was French Canadian. He gave me time to get my strength back and we went back to it again. But the Japanese would've been rougher on us if they found out we had been fighting instead of working."

Frank Grady was an Army cryptographer on Corregidor, was forced to surrender, and had followed the same fate as Simmons by going through Bilibid, Cabanatuan, and then to Japan. He was imprisoned in Yokohoma, south of Niigata. In his book, *Surviving the Day*, Grady explains how survival had been reduced to a base level:

*"...a person had to be determined to live. Those who were not determined to live simply died. I do not exaggerate. Anyone who was unwilling to bend his needs to meet the paucity of camp conditions took ill and soon was dead...Volatile emotions - be they intense fear, hatred of the Japanese, or antagonisms between POWs - could be deadly because they were an energy drain. Many prisoners who indulged in such emotions dwindled and died."*

Simmons echoes those thoughts. "We'd be going along and one of us would be talking and you couldn't tell anything was wrong. Next day he'd be dead. He would just give up. He thought it would be much easier to die."

I asked him what kept him going, why he didn't give up. "I just wanted to come back home. I just wanted to come back. That's all I wanted. Up until near the very end, I was able to not give up."

Prisoners would often form a buddy system with another prisoner, or within a small group. The purpose was communal support. Simmons was part of such a group that contained three or four other men. He was the only one who survived to make it home.

By late 1944 and early 1945, the war was going poorly for the Japanese, which meant retribution against the POWs. Simmons remembers that "when things started going bad for them, that made all the difference in how they treated us. If there was a big battle and a lot of Japanese would get killed, they'd get mean and take it out on us."

That changed on August 6, 1945. Simmons noticed a difference in the attitudes and actions of the guards. "Thank the good Lord for the atomic bomb, because the Japanese really changed when they dropped that thing. Yes, sir, it scared them to death. You could see the fear in them. And we were laughing, saying, 'Come on, drop another one!' We didn't know what had happened, but whatever it was they did, we wanted them to drop another one."

Even so, Simmons had reached the point where he could take no more. He was ready to give up. The months of physical abuse, deprivation and disease had taken its toll. His body was gaunt as his skin hung flimsily from his bones. More importantly, he had finally run out of will. His captors had won. "I had made my mind up that I was not going to work for the Japanese any longer, that it just wasn't right. I was just too weak. Ready to give up is what it was. And I thought, 'Tomorrow, when we line up and count off and get ready to go to work, I'm going to stand right here.' So when I got out there that morning, I said to myself, 'I'm going to stand here and let them leave me.' They would have shot me probably. So we counted off, and just before the time when we would normally have walked off, a Japanese came out there and said the war is over. The Japanese had surrendered.

"I believe in prayer, I always have. I had prayed that the war would be over and I would get to go home again. I just kept praying. Then they announced the surrender and I knew it that quick to thank the Lord that today was the day. I had made all those plans to give up and then that was it."

After word of surrender spread through the prison camps in mid-August, the big question among the POWs became, "What's Next?" MacArthur sent messages over the radio to prisoners telling them to stay in their respective camps until they were liberated by Allied troops. But rumors among the prisoners said that Tokyo was the place to be: Food, showers, women and fun awaited them there. Some reportedly went and found what they were looking for, but Simmons stayed put.

At his camp in Niigata, the first order of business was to relieve the Japanese guards of their swords and weapons, a humiliating submission. "It was our people giving the orders then," smiles Simmons. After a long week in Niigata, Simmons was finally on his way back home. The prisoners marched to downtown Niigata to a train that took them to Tokyo. Simmons laughs about that march and says, "I didn't mind walking downtown to catch that train! I sure didn't mind doing that!"

In Tokyo, the prisoners, ghastly in appearance, were given clean clothes and the first full meal they had had in three and a half years. When Simmons joined the Navy in 1940, he weighed approximately 180 pounds. By the time he arrived in Tokyo he was a walking skeleton, weighing only 97 pounds. His frail condition was standard among POWs emerging from the bleak prison camps throughout southeast Asia.

Bob Simmons was one of the lucky ones. Some 37 percent of all POWs under Japanese command died. Compare that to the 1-2 percent that died in German camps and you begin to realize that the Japanese military not only made Allied POWs suffer, they murdered them through means of starvation and abuse.

From Tokyo Simmons boarded a hospital ship on which nurses tended to and fed him. He says he had no problems reacquainting his body with hearty food again. "I was putting on about 1-2 pounds a day on that ship." After a brief hospital stay in the Philippines, it was back across the ocean he had crossed four years earlier on the doomed *Shark*.

Simmons and hundreds of other prisoners from Niigata arrived in Oakland, Calif., in September to no parades or fanfare, only a ride to another hospital. Many men still suffered from the weakening effects of the tropical diseases they had fought since Bataan and Corregidor, in addition to the years of malnutrition. Simmons spent two weeks at a hospital in Oakland, then was flown to Charleston, S.C., where he spent another two weeks in treatment. To this day he continues to be plagued by digestive problems that restrict his diet.

Charleston is where he was finally and joyously reunited with his family, which, according to him, gave him the only special treatment he ever received.

While many prisoners wanted to distance themselves from the military immediately after the war, Simmons stayed in. "I hadn't planned on making a career of it. I had just planned on doing one hitch and that's it. But after I came back there still wasn't much work, so I stayed in the Navy instead of joining the bread lines."

After being granted five months off from duty, Simmons remained in Charleston for the next 12 years, working his way up to the rank of chief. He met his wife there and the two were married less than eight months after his return from Japan. Simmons says he's thankful the two didn't meet before the war. "That would have been something else to worry about. I can't say I didn't worry, but I did a good job of holding that down. Some of the guys did a lot of worrying and they didn't last too long."

After leaving the Navy in 1959, he and his wife moved to Hampton Roads, where Simmons worked for many years in the construction business. He and his wife have two children and four grandchildren.

When Bob Simmons talks about his imprisonment in the Philippines and Japan, he speaks surprisingly at ease of it. "I don't mind talking about it. I've talked about it in front of the church. It doesn't take anything away from me. I'm here to tell about it. A lot of guys aren't."

A large part of his acceptance of what happened to him comes from his amazing ability to forgive. He points to his Toyota Camry in the driveway and says, "That's proof to me that I don't hate. I don't. I just couldn't go on hating them like that. I did for a while, maybe two or three years. But you know, they were doing what they were told to do. So were we. The brutality was unnecessary, but that was their training. The Japanese were good soldiers, good sailors, and good pilots. But I got a lot more of them than they did of me."

Fifty-five years later, part of Japan lives on in his speech. He can still carry on a conversation in Japanese, which is an odd sounding mixing of cultures since it's spoken in his country-boy accent.

Naturally, one would think his ordeal as a POW would be Simmons' biggest life event, his turning point. Yet he points to another time, only a moment really. It took place on the *Mary Anne* off the coast of Bataan when they were under heavy Japanese fire. "It was like there was this big screen that was in front of me, and on it I could see everything I had done wrong. And I told the Lord that if I cold get through that I was going to be a different man. I've tried to do that. I could have done better, I guess."

According to my mother, Bob Simmons has kept the promise he made to himself. Our family has known the Simmons for years, and in that time he has shown himself to be someone not bitter about the cruelties inflicted upon him, but someone who has reached out through his faith in God to those around him. My mother states that the true amount of his generosity in terms of time and money will never be known. How a man can have so much taken from him, yet give so much, is a testament to the power of forgiveness, faith, and the sheer will of not giving up.

# HOMER CHARLES MINNIE

1937                                                      2000

Charlie Minnie is one of the Navy's old salts. He has been around the world at least twice on voyages that have been a mixture of fear and adventure. He was driven to the military by the promise of steady pay and regular meals. But the pay would seem little and the meals would turn thin as the demands of the upcoming war years approached. And as those war years drew closer, Charlie Minnie would find himself in an almost forgotten fleet that made it only through the first three months of World War II.

When he joined the Navy in the mid-1930s, there was no war for America, but the embers of war were burning. Japan had invaded China, Hitler was building a war machine, and fascists were leading a revolt in Spain. It was the uprising in Spain that first brought the farm-raised Minnie across the Atlantic. He served aboard a ship that ferried American refugees out of Spain and into France. From his service there, he has a one-of-a-kind souvenir. Under a glass frame lies a small, crudely stitched American flag with a short description of its origin. The story tells of the American Ambassador to Spain and his wife who were trying to flee the brutality of Gen. Francisco Franco. They were told that if they were caught on the roads without American credentials, they would be shot. During the night before their escape to meet the Navy ship on which Minnie served, the ambassador's wife hastily stitched a small cloth flag that they placed on the grill of the car, allowing them safe passage. As a member of the crew that pulled the couple's car aboard, Minnie slipped the flag into his pocket, and now shows it off proudly.

But nothing matches the pride, or reverence, that he shows for one of America's most forgotten fleets, the Asiatic Fleet. A small mix of World War I ships that had been dispatched to Asian waters in the early 1920s, the Asiatic Fleet served primarily in diplomatic and rescue roles in China, Japan, and Russia. In the 1920s it was an impressive, effective deterrent. By the 1940s the Asiatic Fleet was a vulnerable and unprepared target for the flag of Japan that would unfurl across the Pacific.

Soon after Japan began its expansionist saber rattling, Minnie was assigned to the aging Asiatic Fleet. Shortly after he and his shipmates arrived in China, they were forced to move south to the Philippines as the Japanese stormed through southern China. Then Pearl Harbor was attacked. In a matter of hours, the World War I-era Asiatic Fleet was on the scrambled edge of America's defenses.

Never was the David and Goliath analogy more appropriate than it was during the Asiatic Fleet's eighty-five days of running and battling at the onset of the war. They fought mainly at night, with little knowledge of their enemy. They had no air cover, no radar, limited ammunition, sparse communications, and repair facilities that were disappearing by the week. All of this against a well-armed, modern Japanese Navy that was honed for war. The Asiatic Fleet had basically come to a gunfight armed with only a knife.

Despite the overwhelming odds the men of the tiny Asiatic Fleet, including Charlie Minnie, fought bravely, even successfully. To their credit is the first American victory of World War II when four of their destroyers sneaked into a Japanese invasion fleet at Balikpapan, Borneo, in January of 1942. Yet, with such odds, losses of men and materials were inevitable. In his book, *The Fleet the Gods Forgot*, Capt. Walter Winslow, a pilot in the Asiatic Fleet, summarizes their plight during the bleak, early days of the war: "*...within a matter of three months' time, the little fleet, manned by courageous Americans short of everything but guts, a fleet whose victories were few but its unsung heroes many, passed without notice into the shadowy recesses of time.*"

It has not passed from Charlie Minnie, though. His memories of those days in the Asiatic Fleet, as well as his return to the Atlantic where he fought against the Germans, are strong and clear. In 2001 he is 85 years old, but his war stories are still sprinkled with the salt of an old-time Navy man. Here's how he told his incredible story to me as we sat in the den of his Suffolk home one bright Sunday afternoon.

"Back in the depression days of 1932 to 1935, things were very rough. I did everything possible during those days to keep from starving to death. So, somebody said you could get thirty dollars a month and a plate of beans every morning and corn bread if you joined the military. To a farm boy in Ohio, that sounded like a fortune to me. So low and behold I went down to the recruiting office in Cincinnati and applied for the Army, Navy, and

Marines. About four days later I got a letter from the Navy. I went down, they gave me a physical, and told me they had a quota for seven men and one of them was sick and he couldn't make it, so I was the seventh. They put me on a train and where do I wind up? Norfolk, Virginia. I had never heard tell of it before. We ended up at the old train station where the baseball field (Harbor Park) is now. We got on a street car which took us to N.O.B (Norfolk Naval Operation Base ). They confiscated all of our luggage we had brought with us because we didn't need it. They put me in a detention unit for three weeks for inoculation shots and this and that. Now, whoever heard of a farm boy who was used to cuddling up in an old feather bed, winding up sleeping in a hammock? And that's what I did for the next several years.

"At the same time, General Franco was taking over Spain. I was in the Fourth Division, which was an armored division, and I was on board the *U.S.S. Raleigh*. We were sent to and stationed at Villefranche, France, which was only about twenty miles from the Italian border, and Monaco was in between. We went down through the Mediterranean into Spain and evacuated 481 refugees. We made about a dozen trips to get American refugees that were over there on business doing this, that and the other, and sightseers. Franco didn't like them so we had to get them out of there. So we took them up to Marseilles, France, and dropped them off. We spent two-and-a-half years there evacuating refugees.

"We had a bachelor admiral. That admiral didn't like sitting up in his cabin all those days, so he'd say, 'Let's weigh anchor and go sight seeing.' I toured every village, every city in the Mediterranean Sea. Some of the sights I saw were out of this world. I saw a volcano blow in Italy. But we saw some of the most awful sites in Oran and Algiers, how the poor people lived. They would take a goat skin and reverse it and dry it out, and use the tail for a spout and sell water. That goat skin would gag a maggot. But anyway, most of those people would have diseases, and they'd have to crawl.

"On May 18, 1938, we were relieved by the *U.S.S. Omaha*, and we went back to the States. We went to the West Coast and wound up in a Hawaiian detachment. Hawaii had about 15 ships, and my ship, the *Raleigh*, wound up as flagship. I spent about two years in Honolulu, and got transferred to the *U.S.S. Parrott*, which was a part of what was called the Asiatic Fleet.

"By 1940, the Asiatic Fleet was still out there in China, and I had never heard tell of that fleet before. They were formed way back in the early 20s. That fleet was to safeguard all American interests that were out there. We had millionaire Americans out there that were in oil and clothing, you name it, any kind of business. And they were showing the Chinese how to make that stuff. So, that's why there was the Asiatic Fleet. We only had thirteen destroyers, and they were four-stack destroyers that were built back in 1919. We were starting to get out of China in 1940 because the Japanese were taking over. So the Fleet came on down to Manila Bay in the Philippines.

"Adm. Hart was Commander in Chief of the Asiatic Fleet. He had sent a message on November 29, 1941, just before Pearl Harbor, to Washington, D.C., stating that hostilities would soon be declared by the Japanese. We had broken their code (the Purple Code), and had found out a lot. Anyway, so far as Washington, D.C., was concerned, they paid no attention to it. Then, on December 5, the *Parrot* went on down to Tarakan, which was on the island of Borneo, southeast of the Philippines. The Dutch had control of that area back then. The land in Tarakan, you could dig a hole thirty feet deep and it would fill up with oil, that's how rich the ground was. The crude coming out of the ground was like thick molasses, and that's the stuff we'd run the ship off of. We had an eight-inch pipe running down the pier and put it into the ship. Now, the more stuff you throw off the ship, the more oil you can carry. Since we didn't know what exactly was going to happen with the Japs, we wanted to get as much of that oil as we could. We had refrigerators on there for ice and this, that and the other. That had to go over the side. We had a whale boat that went over the side because we didn't need it. We basically stripped the ship and loaded up with oil, and stood by.

"Then Pearl Harbor happened, and soon after that the Japs came over and bombed Manila Bay in the Philippines. Then the Japs started coming down into where we were at Tarakan. Now, the Japanese were an awful race. They had sympathy for nobody. I saw a Japanese throw a baby in the air and catch it with his saber. I saw that in Tarakan before we got out. We left out of there scared to death.

"We then made it down to the Dutch East Indies to a little town called Surabaja on Java. It was south of where we had been at Borneo. When we pulled up in there, I noticed that we were unloading all of our health records, supply records, dental records, pay records, the whole bit, and I couldn't understand what was going on. What was going on was that they were sending us to a place called Balikpapan, back there at Borneo, where all those Japs were.

"At Balikpapan, there were thirty-five Jap ships and we could see they had a couple of little tin cans (supply ships) running back and forth. I was the assistant gunnery officer. We went in there in a sneak attack and made a clover leaf through the entire Jap force there. While we were maneuvering, I looked ahead about a half mile, maybe. Now the water out there's real phosphorous, and it makes a white streak when something's going through it. I looked out on the port side and I saw this white streak coming. Torpedo. I said, 'Captain, torpedo's dead on the port beam!' He looked at it and gave that ship a hard fifteen degrees. A torpedo only has a small detonating head, and if it doesn't hit that, it won't go off. So the torpedo came along, hit the side of the fire room, and went right about its business. It left a groove about six feet down that side. A very dear friend of mine was a radioman and he was sitting down just about where it hit. It knocked him out of his chair.

"We sank seven of their ships, us old four-pipe destroyers that were built back around 1920. Anyway, during the course of that, there was a Japanese tanker we saw. Capt. said, 'Fire 1 and fire 3!' for the torpedoes, and the boy running the torpedo switch keeled over backwards and fainted. I hopped off the bridge and pulled the trigger. Out went two fish and sank that tanker. Blew it all to smithereens. On top of the tanker were 150 gallon oil drums, and on top of the oil drums were roughly 400 and some Jap soldiers. The whole works went up into the sky. After that, I threw up over the side. But I got to thinking that war is war, and it's either them or me.

"We ran out of torpedoes and we ran out of ammunition, and we left out of there without a scratch. So, and you'll like this, we pulled back into the pier at Surabaja at daybreak, and Adm. Hart was standing there. He looked up and said, 'What are you doing back here? You were sent on a suicide mission!' My heart dropped. On a suicide mission? I wasn't ready to die.

"There at Surabaya, we cleaned up a bit and rearmed best we could with the meager supplies we had and went into the Battle of the Java Sea. The Japs about annihilated us (five U.S. ships were sunk), but we sank one ship and damaged a couple of others. The Dutch and the English were along with us. I got hit by a piece of shrapnel. It was just a scratch, so I just put a bandage on it and went about my business. This might sound comical, but a bullet came in and cut the ropes holding the whale boat that was back on board, and the boat fell in the water. Meanwhile, on the side of the ship there were three big fifty-gallon cans of gasoline, and that being a fire hazard, we dumped them over the side. One of them only had a little bit of gasoline in it, so it floated. As we made a real hard turn to avoid a Jap ship, a chief petty officer fell over the side. He saw that can of gas floating and went over to it and hung on to it. Then low and behold, there came that whale boat floating at him. And he climbed aboard that boat and some way or another he got that gasoline into it and went on down 130 some miles to Surabaja. When we pulled into Surabaja, there he stood.

"So once again we went back in and repaired as much as possible. Then the Japs had started to come down towards Surabaja. At one of the piers we were at, there was a big metal building at the end of the pier that was full of Hennigans beer from top to bottom. It was Sunday afternoon, and me and this other man were playing Monopoly at the end of the pier and here come the Japanese trying to dive bomb us. Everyone of those bombs went right over the top of us, and the noise would make you sick. It sounds like a jet engine starting up. But one of them hit that beer building and blew Hennigans beer all over everything. Another one hit a great big tree where some natives were working under it. There was five of them. That bomb split that tree and killed everyone of them. For us, there was nowhere to go, so we just sat there and watched the whole thing until they left.

"We made liberty there and a bunch of us had a hotel room in town. About four o'clock in the morning, the madam of the hotel came up to us and said, 'Yanks, you better go home! Look up the street!' About a mile up the road we saw a flock of tanks coming. The Japs had made a landing on the eastern side of Surabaja just down from where we were. We had nothing on but our white pants and we were barefooted, and away we went. We got back to the pier and they were already chopping the lines off from the ship. We shimmied up one of those lines and got aboard ship. That's how close I was to becoming a POW.

"Then it got so bad that Adm. Hart told us to try to get to Australia the best way we knew how. We left out of there with the *Pillsbury* and a couple of other ships. Our ship went east and made a beeline for Darwin, Australia. It was on the northern side of Australia. But the *Pillsbury* and the others went west towards the Indian Ocean, and nobody ever heard another word from them again. Not one word, not one survivor.

"We finally made it down to Perth, Australia, and thought we had made it to heaven. If anybody's ever been to Australia, you'd want to go back a second time, even a third time. Those people down there would give you the shirt right off their back. Very friendly. We stayed there for a while because the Japs didn't dare invade Australia. Instead they went over to places like the Solomon Islands and Guadalcanal. After Perth, we went down to southern Australia to Melbourne to refuel, then headed down to Sydney. And on the way there, low and behold here comes a two-man submarine into Sydney Harbor. The Australians were ready for them and went out there and got that sucker and killed those two Japanese.

"We stayed in Sydney about a week to recuperate a little bit and relax because we hadn't had a decent thing to eat in months and months. We'd had powdered eggs, powdered potatoes, and what we called cpo (chief petty officer) dogs, which were nothing but Vienna sausages. So we about killed ourselves gorging on the food in the restaurants.

"Then we went to a little Polynesian village in the middle of the South Pacific, stayed overnight, got more fuel, then finally pulled back into the Hawaiian Islands. That was about six months after Pearl Harbor, and there were still ships scattered all over the place, still fires burning. It was an awful mess. The bunkhouse I was in before I left had a bomb go right through it and killed a couple of men. That would've been me if I hadn't shipped out.

"I finally made it back to the States, then got sent to the East Coast through the Canal, and came over here to Norfolk with about fifteen other men. We were put with this group that would go out and look for German submarines. We'd cover three-hundred-mile circles all the way to England,

Casablanca, and even to Mermansk, Russia. In Mermansk, the Russians wouldn't let us off the ship even though we were giving them materials. When we left there we went up through the Arctic Circle. It was forty degrees below zero. When you're standing a four-hour watch and drinking coffee, you have to urinate quite a bit. To urinate, you had to do it over the side. If the urine hit the deck, it'd bounce. Frozen. We had parkas up around our faces, and as you breathed, icicles would form around your mouth. Nobody took a bath for thirty days. You didn't dare. Our watches were four hours on and four hours off. And you'd drink so much coffee on your watch that you couldn't ever go to sleep. It was kind of rough.

"We carried about thirty depth charges. You could set them down to fifty feet, one-hundred feet and one- hundred-and-fifty feet. If you got a ping on your sound gear, and it registered one-hundred-and-fifty feet, then you set your depth charge for that. We got one submarine on our first trip. We got the oil slick, but we never did capture anybody.

"Now this really happened, I'll swear on my mother's grave. I was on my watch one night about 11:30 up in the radar pit. And I said, 'Pip on the radar, Captain!' He about tore down the door getting in to look at it. He pressed the general quarters, which means all hands to their battle stations. The pip was about 18,000 yards out, so we crept in, crept in, kept on getting closer and the thing didn't move. This isn't known to the public, but I saw it. When we came up to about a thousand yards, it never moved, it just sat there! So the old man scratched his head and said, 'Somebody's crazy'. He struck the search light, and there lay this monstrous German submarine on the surface, about twice as big as an ordinary submarine. It was what they called a mother sub. They used them to re-supply the U boats and other German ships. They must have thought we were a German ship, so that's why they just sat there waiting for us. So the captain said, 'Commence firing!' We put about ten rounds right through that sub, and down she started. Then we radioed in the next morning to tell them we were going to look for survivors. There were thirty-seven survivors, and each man had a life jacket on that had Goodyear Rubber Co., Akron, Ohio, stamped on the back of them. We had a rope ladder hanging over the side and they would climb aboard. Most of them were very gentlemanly. One man came aboard in a lieutenant's uniform, and I was standing there as junior officer of the deck. He says to me, 'Good afternoon, sir', in perfect English. I said, 'Who might you be?' He said, 'I am an American citizen, born and bred. I went to Harvard University. I'm from Boston. Anything else you'd like to know, I'd be glad to tell you. Where's your commanding officer? I have a lot of information for him.' See, he had gone over to Germany and they put him in the Navy. He gave us about everything he knew about Germany, which gave us an awful lot of insight as to what was going on. We put him in the officer's quarters since he was an American.

"Only a few of the others were real Nazis. The rest were just regular Germans. We put them in the aft part of the ship. We had a quartermaster who spoke German, and he went back to listen to their conversation. The Nazis told the other Germans, 'Any of you make one remark to these Americans and on your way back home after the war, you'll be beheaded.' So, we couldn't get much out of them. And when we tried to talk to this one Nazi, he'd spit in your face. So, when he was being transferred to another ship, we put him on what we called a preacher's pulley. It was a line on a pulley system that you'd shoot over to another ship. Both ships would have to go straight and even to keep the line out of the water. But when that Nazi was going across, we went left, right, left, right, letting that line go all the way down in the water. We'd dunk him and bring him up. Dunk him, bring him up. It almost killed him.

"The Atlantic didn't bother me too much. We were hardened by then. But in the Pacific, you never knew.

"So that's the way I rounded out my war. It left a nervous wreck out of me. I've been sitting in a doctor's chair ever since. Many a night I get up and pace up and down." Mrs. Minnie: "He can't stay in one place. He's gotta keep moving. He has a hard time sleeping every night. The night part has been rough. And when he does sleep, he's talking all kinds of war stories. Half the time I can't understand." Mr. Minnie: "Right now, I take a sleeping pill to go to sleep. Years ago, the Navy didn't care anything about retirees, and I had to go to a civilian doctor. Now, they've opened it up to where I can go over to the Naval Hospital. Some of what has fallen apart in my life was because of that time in the Navy. I lost my first wife. But I never did cry about it."

Instead of crying about it, Charlie Minnie has immersed himself in keeping up with old crew members. He volunteered to organize a reunion of the Asiatic Fleet in 1989. Dozens of men and their wives traveled to Norfolk to be with each other again and tell seldom-heard stories about the "Fleet the Gods Forgot".

In his mid-eighties, his habits from the depression still echo. Only a few days before I met with him, he had just planted four rows of Vidalia onions, and was planning on planting his potatoes the next week. "Where I come from, if you didn't have a garden, you starved to death." His doctors tell him he shouldn't be bending over to work in his garden, but he refuses to sit idle. He still approaches each day with the same determination he did more than sixty years ago. Part of that determination is for others to not forget the sacrifices he and so many others made. He sums it up by saying, "If it wasn't for us, you might be seeing the flag of Japan instead of the stars and stripes. Wouldn't that be something."

1950

2000

George Bergmann usually glosses over the first seven years of his life just to make them easier to explain. But after hearing the entire story, one comes to realize what could have been a very different outcome to this man's life.

His full name is George Herrman Von Bergmann. His ancestry is 100 percent German. Both his parents were born and raised in Germany, and his father even fought against the Americans during World War I. But during the 1920s, as Germany reeled from a crashing economy, Adolf Hitler was beginning his rise in German politics. Col. Bergmann, George's father, grew to hate Hitler, viewing him as a thug. As Hitler's popularity and power slowly began to rise, and labor and social conditions continued to fall, Col. Bergmann felt it best to move his family to America.

In the late 1920s he immigrated with his daughter and wife, then pregnant with George. But only months after arriving at Ellis Island, the elder Bergmann died of illnesses related to mustard gas poisoning he suffered during World War I. One of his last requests was to have his ashes scattered in New York Harbor off the Staten Island ferry. He wanted nothing more to do with the Germany for which he had once fought. By then young George Bergmann had been born an American citizen.

It is at this point in the new immigrant's life that things begin to take on the twists that are the fodder for books and movies. Bergmann's mother, with no husband to support them, sent him and his older sister back to Germany to live with their grandparents until she could find a husband in America to support the family. Almost seven years would pass before that would happen.

During that time Bergmann became a part of the new nationalism that was sweeping Germany. Promising "Freedom and Bread," Adolf Hitler brought hope to a floundering Germany. Bergmann still recalls his grandfather taking him to see Hitler at the coliseum in Berlin. "I thought Hitler was a hero," says Bergmann. "When you're seven years old you'll 'Seig Heil!' (Hail Victory!) to anyone." In fact, he seig heiled quite a bit as a member of the German Junior Youth, a program for boys under the age of nine. Bergmann compares it to the Cub Scouts. "Back then, it was a positive thing. But it turned into something very different towards the beginning of the war." Bergmann was on his way down the misguided path that most German boys would follow during the years to come.

Going back to America no longer seemed a good idea to young George. "When we would see a plane, which you didn't see a lot of in those days, my grandmother, my umma, would say, 'Look, that's your mother coming back to take you away from me.' I'd run inside and hide because I didn't want to go. I loved my umma and she loved me."

But Bergmann's mother did send for him and his sister. In 1933 he was back in Brooklyn. He was born there, but everything inside him had become German.

Bergmann did not find the love from his mother that he did from his grandparents. He claims his mother was a staunch German disciplinarian partial to using a belt on a bare bottom. The one thing she did have in common with his grandparents was her zeal for Hitler. "When I went to the movies with her, they'd show those news clips of Hitler before the movie. The other people in the audience would boo and hiss, but my mother would clap. I'd try to sink down in my seat."

As Bergmann spent his school years in Brooklyn becoming Americanized, war broke out across Europe. Adolf Hitler, the same man he had saluted and said 'Seig Heil!' to a few years before, was the spark under the flames that would soon engulf Bergmann's homeland. The same nationalistic fever that had years before swept through Germany was now moving across America. But this time Bergmann was on the other side.

In early 1944, at age 16 and eager to get out from under his mother's harsh thumb, he tried to enlist in the Marines. They soon learned that he was underage and he was quickly escorted home by a New York City police officer. George feared another belt lashing from his mother, but instead she signed an underage consent form, allowing George to enlist in the United States Navy. After enlisting, the Navy asked if he would have problems "killing Germans," especially since his grandparents were still there. "I told them I didn't know, I had never killed a German before, or any one else." Bergmann was promptly assigned to the Pacific, with a restricted classification that would haunt him through his years in the Navy.

From the concrete of Brooklyn, Bergmann's home for the next year and a half was the steel of the *Wilkes-Barre*, a Cleveland Class light cruiser (eight of this class of ship were built in Newport News during the war). After her shakedown cruise on the Chesapeake Bay late in 1944 she set off through the Panama Canal and into what would become some of the bloodiest fighting in the Pacific.

Bergmann's primary duty station was that of a water tender, which meant he checked and adjusted pressure gauges below deck. He was part of what was known as the "black gang" or the "bilge rats." "We were called that because we were always down in the engine room, so we didn't take too many showers, maybe once a week if we needed it. A lot of civilians thought the black gang was made up of black people, but there were only about ten blacks on the ship, and they were segregated. They were made to sleep in the bow of the boat, where you got a lot of rocking. We just didn't think much about that kind of stuff back then. And back then, no one said they were African-American or whatever, they were just Americans. I was born in Germany, but I'm not German-American. I'm American."

With the exception of infrequent ports, the ship was a sailor's entire universe. It was there, twenty-four hours a day, that they worked and fought. Movies and mail were hot commodities. Since new movies were hard to get in the middle of the Pacific Ocean, the same movies were seen over and over. "They'd put up a bed sheet on the ship's fantail. I learned that some of the old salts would sit on the other side of the sheet because they said it looked like a different movie from the back."

Bergmann also likes to tell the story of how some of the crew would sit on the trough-style head (toilet) and pass letters from home to one another. Since mail would arrive only once every two weeks, letters were read over and over. Another crew member's letters offered a nice change. "I had friends that would let me read letters from their mothers or their wives. They really did. And I'd listen to guys talk about how they missed home, because there was love there, but I didn't have that. I was jealous that I didn't have that emotion. I didn't have anyone waiting for me."

During their first few months at sea, the only thing Japanese the *Wilkes-Barre* sailors saw were survivors of Japanese radar picket boats sunk by alert U.S. destroyers. But in just eight months the "Willie-Bee" would have four battle stars under her belt, and would be in place to view one of the war's most glorious moments.

In early January, 1945, her first battle star was awarded for her support of Navy squadrons that struck Formosa, Luzon, and the China Coast. Iwo Jima was next. On February 19, Marines left their transports and headed towards the black beaches of Iwo Jima. Some 20,000 Japanese awaited them. By nightfall, 566 Marines were dead. By the end of the operation, 6,821 Americans died on the island. Of the 20,000 Japanese soldiers, only 1, 083 survived. During the height of the battle the "Willie Bee" was called in to bolster the shore bombardment of the island with her six-inch guns. By having her fire directed by spotters in planes called Kingfishers (some of which were launched from the *Wilkes-Barre*), she helped demolish enemy gun positions, pillboxes, fortified caves and ammunition dumps. She was given a thanks from the Marines ashore for turning back a Japanese counterattack.

Bergmann's battle station was that of a hot-shell man on one of the big 38 mm guns used for shore bombardment. The hot-shell man was the guy who caught the hot expended shell casing (they wore asbestos gloves), then threw it down a small hole within the gun mount. If the shell didn't make it down the hole, Bergmann would have to fish it out because it would interfere with the gun spinning around properly. "I was called all kinds of names when those shells didn't make it down that hole."

Since Bergmann's 38 mm was a closed mount (both closed and open mounts were used), there was little time, or even possibility, of stopping to see what was going on in battle. "There was none of this, 'Gee, I think I'll stick my head up because I'd really like to see the enemy planes'. And something they don't show you in the movies is sometimes you piss in your pants from being scared. It's a human thing to be scared."

Okinawa was the next big step in the island-hopping campaign that would draw the Allies closer to homeland Japan. The island was viewed as the base from which assault troops could stage and train for the attack on the Japanese mainland. As American troops launched the invasion of Okinawa on Easter Sunday, April 1, 1,300 ships, including the *Wilkes-Barre*, gathered offshore. It was the largest and final U.S. amphibious assault of the war. It was also the costliest. Some 15, 946 Americans (Army, Marines, U.S. Pacific Fleet) were killed in the operation. Japanese losses were enormous: 107, 539 killed.

Okinawa turned out to be a harrowing time for Bergmann and the rest of the crew because of the Kamikaze (Divine Wind) Corps. Of the 2, 257 suicide missions that Japan hurled at the American fleet during its last desperate months of the war, 1, 465 came during Okinawa. In all, 30 U.S. ships were destroyed, 164 others damaged. Adm. "Bull" Halsey later said that the kamikaze was, "the only weapon I feared in the war."

The *Wilkes-Barre* was one of the lucky ones. She came under heavy kamikaze attacks but was never hit. In fact, she racked up eight confirmed kills. "When the kamikazes were coming at you, they tried to have the sun behind them so it was harder to see them. For the planes that weren't kamikazes, that were broadside to the ship heading towards the carriers or bigger destroyers, you didn't actually have to hit them. The shrapnel would spread out and hit the plane. But for the kamikaze, you had to hit that son of a bitch. You're not going to scare him away. He wanted to commit suicide."

And many did with devastating results. A *Wilkes-Barre* crew member's journal gives us an idea of what it was like as kamikazes plunged from the sky:

## March 11 1945

*Air defense sounded at about 0200, and a lone Bogie was coming in on our port bow. We opened up between eight and ten thousand yards, and the plane turned to the right after coming in as close as four thousand yards. No results observed. Air defense sounded again at 0845, and the Bogie came within 15 miles before being splashed by Combat Air Patrol. Condition 1E was set, and we lounged around our battle stations. Possibly 10 minutes later, a lone plane came out of the clouds at about 1500 feet altitude from our port quarter and passed astern of us at great speed. As the plane passed our stern we were able to see that it was a Zeke, and had come in on us unnoticed by lookouts and with no warning from our radar. We could see the red circle insignia on the wings. Not a single ship in the task force was aware of this single enemy plane in our midst, which dove on the Bunker Hill (a carrier) without a shot being fired at it. It struck aft of amidships in a huge column of fire and smoke, setting fire to the planes parked on the flight deck and hangar deck. A moment later, a second Jap plane came sneaking in...It too was a Zeke, and our 20 and 40 mms opened up on it as it began its dive on the Bunker Hill. Our fire hit the plane, and she began to burn on her way down, but the hits were not hard enough to knock the plane off the dive, for it struck amidships just forward of where the first plane had hit, and a second huge explosion occurred. The carrier was now a mass of flame and smoke from the superstructure to the stern...It was a tremendous sight to see, and a terrifying one, too. We watched through binoculars as men went over the side to escape the heat and flames... Meanwhile, Combat Air Patrol reported another Bogie on the way in. A Zeke was coming in fast and we opened up. The plane veered slightly and came in on us at high speed. Already I had visualized the same thing happening to us as had just occurred to the Bunker Hill. But a moment later the plane was hit, and plunged into the sea in a satisfying spume of water.*

Some 372 men were killed and 264 wounded on the *Bunker Hill*. The *Wilkes-Barre* was immediately called to help put out the fire and aid in any way possible. Burial services for fifteen of those killed were held on the *Wilkes-Barre* as the dead were slipped into the sea from underneath American flags. Bergmann and his fellow crew stood on deck and saluted the dead. "That was the closest we had come to seeing mortal combat. Everything was in the distance up to that point. It made me realize how close to death we could be."

The bloody fighting on and around Okinawa finally ended after two months. From early July to mid-August, Bergmann and his fellow crew were called upon for shore bombardment of Japanese industrial areas, preparing for the final invasion of Japan, Operation Olympic, set for November 1, 1945. Even though the war had ground on for almost four years by this time, Bergmann says his hatred for the Japanese never waned. "We were reminded constantly of the Bataan Death March and Pearl Harbor. We went in there to kill Japs and to get even for those that went down in Pearl Harbor. I would still get tears in my eyes because I knew those men were down there."

That final invasion, of course, never happened. The age of atomic warfare had forced Japan into an unconditional surrender after the second bomb was dropped on Nagasaki. On September 2, 1945, V-J Day, surrender ceremonies were held aboard the *USS Missouri* in Tokyo Bay, and George Bergmann was there. The 17-year-old kid, who could have just as easily fought for Hitler, was there as part of the armada of American vessels to escort the *Missouri*... just in case. Bergmann echoed the thinking that the Japanese were not beyond launching a surprise attack during the signing ceremonies, because in his words, "They liked dying." Tensions were high amid the fleet, as noted by one of the *Wilkes-Barre* crew members:

## 2 September

*It hardly seems possible that it is all over and all the useless waste and killing is going to stop. We all held our breath for a minute and were very suspicious when the Japanese signatory looked at his watch and hesitated several times before he signed. We had visions of a last suicide fling of some kind such as a kamikaze plane aimed at the Missouri's quarterdeck with all of those high officials present. We have all seen their treachery and killing and would put nothing past them. I guess they realize though that one slip and Japan would be reduced to dust. At any rate, we breathed much easier when it was over.*

The "Willie-Bee" was positioned a quarter mile away, and while officers watched the proceedings with binoculars, most of the crew, including Bergmann, listened to a play-by-play, baseball-style, on the radio. He was below decks but was able to catch a glimpse of the ships in Tokyo Bay through a small porthole. Bergmann says that although V-J Day was a great day, the crew wasn't as excited as they had been a few weeks earlier when the word of surrender first spread among the fleet. They had already had their party. And believe it or not, he says he even felt a hint of sadness on that day for personal reasons. "This sounds crazy, but for me it was kind of sad when it was over because that meant I had to go home. I feared my mother more than I did the Japs, because I had never seen a Jap, but I had seen my mother."

After the war, Bergmann saw very little of his family or Brooklyn ever again. He stayed on the *Wilkes-Barre* until it was decommissioned in 1947. It was "deep sixed" and is now serving as an artificial underwater reef in the Florida Keys. He served on nine other ships that took him to Bermuda, Korea, and Vietnam. On those ships he became a gun captain for one of the 20 mm antiaircraft guns because, he says, "I was excellent at leading planes. The captain even told me that." He also served as ship's barber, and became the senior ship serviceman in charge of many of the Navy Exchange services.

After serving his 20, he retired from the Navy and went on to be a record-breaking insurance manager, working in Maryland, Pennsylvania, and Hampton Roads. " I had a way of reading people," he recalls. He then moved to Panama and worked as a boilermaker and warehouse supervisor on the Canal until 1987. He says he was there long enough "to learn enough Spanish to get me into trouble, and not enough to get me out." He even worked as a bodyguard for a gun dealer to Iraq. He's been married and divorced four times, has three children and ten grandchildren. His kids tell him they should make a movie about his life. Bergmann thinks Jack Nicholson would be the perfect actor to portray him. Nicholson would have a lot of material with which to work.

Now, in 2001, I look around the room he has labeled the "Memorabilia Room." It is truly that. There's a picture of his father in his German uniform. A complete set of National Geographic magazines dating back to 1914 is neatly stacked around the room. His four battle stars are in view of art from all over South America. Maps of his travels, dancing trophies, sales awards, and even a few bottles of odd sounding liquors line the walls and shelves.

But Bergmann owes most of his adventures to his service in the war. "It was the most exciting thing that ever happened to me. It got me out of the house, out of Brooklyn. And then I think of all the people I've met, and the places I've been. There's no such thing as a good war, but it opened a lot of doors for me."

In his mid-70s, his speech is unapologetically salty as he talks about how he views things nowadays. He doesn't think that kids have any kind of appreciation for what his generation did during World War II. "The younger generation doesn't know crap about us. They don't teach anything about World War II anymore. It's not the Civil War, you know. It didn't happen over a hundred years ago. Up in Wilkes-Barre, Pennsylvania, I met some kids that didn't even know they had a ship named after them. And with four battle stars, any city would be proud to be represented by my ship."

Our country is certainly proud, and so is George Herrman Von Bergmann. He's been a member of the American Legion for over fifty years, a membership feat only one percent of members can boast. But boasting is not what he's about. "We didn't say we needed recognition. It was our duty to serve our country. Everybody was doing something in the war. They were doing their part. It wasn't just for the soldiers, it was for everybody."

1944                                                2001


Imet Neil Van Pelt in a Wal-Mart parking lot. Actually, I followed him there. At a stop light I noticed the car in front of mine had the lettering WW II BB35 CL65, signifying ships served on in World War II. Beside that was a small American flag. Recognizing the driver as someone proud of his service during the war, I followed him a short distance to the parking lot. After I introduced myself and told him about this book, he mentioned that he had a wonderful collection of photos and documentation that I might be interested in seeing. It turned out to be the most professional, extensive, and fascinating chronicle of an individual's war years I have seen. Almost as interesting was the inspiration behind it.

Archibald Douglas Van Pelt was Neil Van Pelt's grandfather. He fought in the Civil War on the side of the South. Neil Van Pelt has a photo of his grandfather in his Confederate uniform, and even has his Confederate pistol. Using this as the introduction to his own story, the younger Van Pelt wrote, "How interesting it would have been if my grandfather had just made some notes for all of us to read and to enjoy." Not wanting his own grandchildren to echo those same thoughts, he decided to spend months putting together memories and lessons from what proved to be a remarkable story. His grandchildren are lucky to have such a treasure.

Neil Van Pelt's lineage to war also extends to his father who served in the Richmond Light Infantry Blues, the forerunner to today's National Guard, in

World War I. Fortunately the war ended before he was sent overseas, and he returned to Richmond, where Neil was born. Neil grew up in Richmond but loved coming to Virginia Beach to see the ocean. He saw more than he wanted to on one such trip.

On June 15, 1942, the Battle of the Atlantic came to Hampton Roads. On that day, Van Pelt and thousands of other beach-goers witnessed the explosion of two tankers one to two miles off the Virginia Beach oceanfront. The tankers were the victims of a mine field laid by a German U-boat. Just a few months later, Van Pelt would cross those same waters.

"I knew it wouldn't be too long before I was drafted. It could have been another six to eight months before I got my notice, but I decided I wanted to go into the Navy. I didn't want the Army. I had always been interested in the water, and was used to it since our family had a house on Gwynn's Island (near Mathews, Virginia)."

He enlisted in August 1942 and was immediately sent to the Naval Training Station in Great Lakes, Illinois. From there he was sent to the Naval Receiving Station in Norfolk where he was assigned to the battleship *USS Texas*. The *Texas* was one of the World War I carryovers. Commissioned in 1914, she was built in Newport News. Although she's now moored at LaPorte, Texas, as a war memorial, she's thought to be seaworthy to this day, which says something about the way they build ships in Newport News. Her history was a proud one, having been present at the surrender of the German Navy in 1918. When the next war with the Germans broke out, she was reworked with updated armor and sent into battle again.

By October, Van Pelt and the rest of the *Texas* crew were leaving the Chesapeake Bay and leading the largest convoy ever assembled up to that point in the war. On his first trip across the Atlantic the memory of those exploding tankers became reality as word of a U-boat contact rifled through the convoy. "That was frightening because I didn't know what to expect. We went to battle stations and it hit me, 'Are we going to get hit?' But that got to be routine after a while." Although the *Texas* went unscathed, approximately 3,500 Allied ships were victims of U-boats during the course of the war.

Since he enlisted with no special qualifications, Van Pelt was assigned to the deck force. Many would say it is still the worst job anyone could have in the Navy. The deck force was the group that did much of the hard labor on the ship. "After a few days of that, I thought there had to be something better to do," he jokes.

He was able to talk his way into administration, which got him off the deck. He then learned that if he could learn how to type he would qualify for a position in the navigation department. So he crafted a piece of cardboard to look like that of a typewriter keyboard. He became a proficient typist quickly, then took and passed the test that allowed him to be reassigned as a navigator's yeoman, third class. His primary job was to type the ship's logs and navigator's reports. It allowed him access to a lot of information that many of the other men on the ship didn't have. "It was a good deal, as far as there could have been a good deal on a ship. I was living the life of Riley."

By late 1942 the Allies were invading North Africa and the *Texas* was ordered into action. It was the crew's first battle of the war. There were numerous German shore batteries that the Army wanted eliminated near Morocco, so the *Texas* opened up with her fourteen-inch guns, did her job, and moved on. After that the crew spent most of 1943 and into mid-1944 running convoys of troops and supplies to and from Scotland, Ireland, Gibraltar, and North Africa. They also made a few trips back home to the States. Van Pelt says the weather was sometimes more of a threat than U-boats. "There were times in the North Atlantic during storms that the whole bow would go under. The ship would pitch so much from port and starboard that we took water all over the topside. That was an old ship, and she really wasn't built like they are nowadays to take the heavy seas. But it did its job."

By June of 1944 the long-awaited invasion of Europe was at hand. The *Texas* would have a front-row seat. Only four days before D-Day, Gen. Dwight Eisenhower, Supreme Commander of Allied Expeditionary Forces, came aboard the *Texas* to give an inspiring pep talk to the crew. They would be expected to come dangerously close to the Normandy coast to give the troops support by knocking out German shore batteries. Their targets would be along the now infamous Omaha Beach.

Van Pelt says that by the early morning hours of June 6, they were fully aware of the enormity of their task, and that anxiety ran deep, mainly due to the weather. Because of low clouds that shrouded the beaches, most ships were forced to rely only on radar (a new invention at that time) for navigation and gunnery data. "The weather had been really bad and it still wasn't good that day. We lost a lot of soldiers going in on the small boats because the water was so rough. Some of them drowned, they lost ammunition, so they were sitting ducks when they got to the beach, the ones that got there."

He also adds that there was concern over hitting our own troops. "It was a good possibility. When the Army wired us that day thanking us for supporting them, we were a little bit surprised because we didn't know if we were doing them much good or not." Doing them much good was an understatement. The *Texas* knocked out nineteen of its twenty-one targets, helping prevent the Germans from moving reinforcements to the beachhead. As German soldiers became overwhelmed, thousands surrendered and were put on ships headed back to England. Some were temporarily jailed on the *Texas*. Surprisingly, their reception on board was not met with boos and hisses, according to Van Pelt. "We were just so curious. It was all so new to us, we just hung around and looked."

Keeping a diary on board ship was strictly forbidden during the war, but for some sailors the historic invasion of Normandy was too tempting not to record. Only five diaries are currently known from the invasion, including one from a Texas crew member.

## 5:45 A.M. (6 June)

*We have now reached our station, 12,000 yards off the coast of France and have dropped anchor. We are preparing to fire the main battery and the second battery in a bombardment in which the first broadside is supposed to be fired at 10 minutes to 6 A.M. and is supposed to continue until 6:30 A.M. which is the hour our troops hit the beach.*

*The time is now 10 minutes to 6 A.M. Tuesday morning. There goes our first broadside with a terrific blast and the battle is on...We have an immediate radio report from our first broadside and our first target was completely destroyed by our first salvo. Our first target was a 6-inch coast artillery gun mounted in a casemate of 15 foot concrete. The report from our spotting plane said we scored a bulls eye hit and our first target was completely blown to hell and a lot of the master race went with it..All of us topside sailors are over on the starboard side of the ship because the ship is firing from the port side. We have our ears full of cotton and are laying on the deck or sitting in some corner and really getting the hell shook out of us. I never heard such a damn noise in all of my life, and I don't ever expect to again either...*

The accuracy of the shelling was not enough to prevent carnage on the beaches. Of the thousands wounded on June 6, dozens of wounded Rangers were brought aboard the *Texas* for transfer to medical facilities. Naval losses were fortunately light, though. Of the 5,333 ships and landing craft involved in D-Day, only a few were sunk due to enemy fire. Yet in the few days following, several more would be sunk due to mines, shelling, and U-boats.

After four days off the Normandy coast, the *Texas* sailed back to Plymouth, England, to reload for the battle that would give Van Pelt the scare of his life. The Battle of Cherbourg began on June 19. Cherbourg was a small town in France that served as a port on a peninsula just to the northwest of where our troops came ashore on D-Day. The Army divisions that landed on Utah Beach were then ordered to attack and seize the town. Once again, the *Texas*, other battleships, destroyers, and cruisers were ordered into the area to knock out German harbor gun emplacements. This time the going wouldn't be so easy.

As a navigator's yeoman, Van Pelt's battle station was on the navigation bridge manning a set of phones that were most often connected to the engine room. "A typical message from the captain for me to relate to the engine room might be, 'Tell the engine room to go to flank speed immediately,' which meant go to maximum speed."

On June 25 the *Texas* was perilously close to the cliffs that lined the shore of Cherbourg, which meant she was within firing range of the German guns. As the Germans fired shell after shell, they seemed to be getting a bead on the ship. Some 65 times those shells straddled the ship as near misses. During the barrage, Van Pelt was sent with the navigator and a few others to leave the navigation bridge and report to the conning tower to man another set of phones for emergency standby. The conning tower is just below the navigation bridge and is used as a backup in case the navigation bridge is knocked out. That was about to happen. The *Texas* took a dead hit to the top of the conning tower only fifteen minutes after Van Pelt arrived there. He was uninjured, only because the explosion shot upwards into the navigation bridge. The 36-inch shell ripped the bridge apart, killing the helmsman and critically wounding several others. The man who had just taken Van Pelt's place lost a leg. Two others, whom Van Pelt had been standing next to, lost legs as well. Another man took serious injuries to much of his body. Van Pelt lost track of him after his injuries, but was able to locate him in the early 1990s, and the two continue to correspond.

"I never will forget that. It was bad enough when you got hit with the concussion, and all the injuries to the guys. What also struck me was that they must have us in range." And the Germans did. The *Texas* took another hit to the port bow. Miraculously, the three-foot shell didn't explode and no major damage was done to the ship. During all of this, a number of fires had started around the main gun turrets due to the intense heat from the constant firing. The crew hurried to push extra ammunition overboard to avoid any major explosions.

For the next three hours the *Texas* battled the German shore batteries while working its way through one of the heaviest mine fields on the French coast. "We were tremendously thankful for the mine sweepers who ironically wired us the following message, 'Thanks for staying in there and taking all the slugging.' The point was that Jerry wasn't wasting time on smaller mine sweepers when they had a big, fat battleship as a target. Then the Army wired us saying, 'Thanks for all the help keeping the shore batteries busy while we advanced inland.'" The Navy's heavy artillery has been credited with shortening by weeks the amount of time required to take Cherbourg.

The war would be over in Europe less than a year after the Battle of Cherbourg. Van Pelt says he and many others thought it would last much longer. "I don't think even our leaders at that point thought that would happen. In fact, from what I've read, they thought the tide might even have been turning, until they really established a foothold over there."

But the foothold was there to stay, so America then began to focus it's resources and troops toward Japan.

That shift to the Pacific included Van Pelt. Near the end of 1944, the *Texas* was back in New York City, and Van Pelt was on a troop train heading across the U.S. "I don't remember much about that trip, but I do remember that we stopped in Ogden, Utah. We had a layover there for about an hour and I had the best steak there I ever had in my life. At least I thought that then." Shortly after that steak dinner, he was in Oceanside, California, for training in ship-to-shore communications and code deciphering techniques.

The war in the Pacific was a very different war from the one he had just left. The strategy, terrain, and climate were all different. Most of all, the enemy was different. Van Pelt states that he felt more hatred for the Japanese than he did for the Germans, mainly because they attacked us. In fact, there was likely no greater hatred of another people during that time than that felt for the Japanese by the Americans. The only animosity to rival it would be the loathing the Russians had for the Germans.

Van Pelt's transfer to the Pacific came in early 1945, when some of the bloodiest fighting was yet to be fought. Van Pelt was transferred to the cruiser *Pasadena* from the cruiser *Springfield* off the coast of Okinawa. He was assigned to administration, yet his battle station was once again that of manning the phones for emergency communication, much like he did on the *Texas*.

When Van Pelt boarded the *Pasadena*, the battle for Okinawa had been raging for over a month, and the kamikazes were racking up large numbers of dead or wounded American servicemen. Van Pelt says that was by far the worst part of being in the Pacific. "It wasn't too frightening at first, after you got over the initial few days of it. But then, when they kept on and on, it got to the point that it was kind of getting to me. I was thinking that somewhere along the line our luck was going to run out." It never did. The *Pasadena* had several close misses, but the kamikazes never claimed their ship or any of the crew. The only recorded loss was that of a pilot from one of the *Pasadena's* spotter planes.

After Okinawa, the *Pasadena* took part in driving the enemy out of the Philippines. The crew then moved on to raid mainland Japan. They shelled places with names like Honshu, Hokkaido, Nakaishi, and Shikoku. From her work in the Pacific, the *Pasadena* was named one of the five best shooting cruisers in the fleet, earning five battle stars.

But of his days in the Pacific, Van Pelt remembers one vividly. On August 5, 1945, the *Pasadena* was ordered to withdraw about 100 miles from the coast of Japan. The crew knew something big was up, but not until a few days later did they know what. On August 6, Hiroshima received the world's first atomic bomb attack, and Van Pelt was glad to hear that it had happened. Like many in the military at the time, he thought the war would drag on for months, perhaps longer. An invasion of Japan seemed to be just a matter of time, and American casualties were forecast to be extreme. But a week later Nagasaki received the next atomic hit, (the *Pasadena* was out of range due to its raids in the northern Japanese islands) and Japan was forced to surrender on August 15. Yet, even after Japan had accepted the Potsdam Surrender terms, kamikaze attacks continued for four more days until word spread to all Japanese troops.

Due to her service record in the Pacific, the *Pasadena* was asked to be part of the American presence in Tokyo Bay on September 2, V-J Day, the end of World War II. Not only was she present, she had the honor of being one of the closest ships to the *Missouri*, where the surrender would officially be signed. This afforded Van Pelt one of the best seats on the bay. "People always see the pictures of hundreds of sailors on the *Missouri*, and it would look like you'd never get a chance to see anything that was happening over there. But I was fortunate in that I had access to a pair of binoculars and it was almost like being aboard the *Missouri*." He says he could easily see the anguished expressions of the Japanese signatories and the stern, proud visage of MacArthur.

After the signing, as the American occupation moved onto Japan, *Pasadena* crew members were allowed shore leave in Tokyo. The day after the surrender, Van Pelt set foot on the Japanese homeland in what seemed to be an empty city. He recalls that the first few days ashore, very few Japanese civilians came out of their homes. They were afraid that their conquerors would hurt them in some way. After all, the beastly Americans had bombed their cities unmercifully for weeks. But as the Japanese people realized that they would be treated fairly and with honor, more and more left the shelter of their homes with each passing day.

"I never really had a lot of hatred for the Japanese people, but I did their leaders. I think the people were brainwashed by them. And part of that brainwashing was that Americans were terrible people."

After seven weeks in Tokyo, Van Pelt was on his way back across the Pacific, back across the U.S., and finally back in Richmond. He was discharged honorably from his naval service in late November 1945. It was a service that put him in the middle of two of the 20th century's most historic moments: D-Day and V-J Day. He had been one of the lucky ones. He got to go home.

In 2001, he is in his late 70s. He has five children and five grandchildren. They will all have the chance to know him just a little bit better because of the work he has put into recording his service in the Navy. His memories of the war and his dedication to keeping those memories alive are strong. That dedication is rooted in the emotion that swept the country fifty-five years earlier. "There was a lot of patriotism back then, an awful lot of patriotism. Not just in the service, but also in the workers who were making things for the troops. I think there was more patriotism then than there has been since, and may ever be again."

That sense of purpose made Van Pelt's decision to enlist and serve an easy one. "We didn't have any choice, and we didn't want any choice. We knew we had to do it. That's all. I never gave it a second thought."

1940

2000

Leo Milam is the first man I ever met who joined the military because he thought it was a safer job than the one he had before. He made it through twenty-two years in the United States Navy, but says he may not have made it another day in the mountains of West Virginia. By age 50 he had outlived most of those that stayed behind, crouched in the tunnels of dusty, perilous coal mines.

Milam grew up in a house owned by the coal company that ran the town and the town's economy. As Appalachia withered under the Great Depression, money, food, and clothing were precious commodities. Milam's family grew their own food and his mother worked hard to keep the kids in school as long as possible. But she couldn't afford to put both Leo and his sister through high school. One had to drop out. The decision was easy. Most girls were thought to need an education, but the boys were the ones that needed the job. And in Coal River, West Virginia, that job was working in the mines. At 17, Leo quit high school and went into the mines to ferret out the black rock. The work was hard and the living was short. "Most of the time you didn't live to be but thirty-five or forty years old," Milam says. "So I figured that after two tops falling in, why I better get out if I'm going to live."

Getting out meant joining the Navy in 1940. He laughs as he recalls, "I had no idea what the Navy was all about. But I couldn't believe I was getting in a place where they'd feed you three times a day and give you a place to sleep and then pay you on top of that. I knew somebody was crazy!"

He was put on a train headed for Norfolk, then a ship headed for the Pacific. "The day I walked on a ship is the day I felt like I had found a new home. But when we pulled out of Norfolk we ran into a big storm around Cape Hatteras and I had to get over my seasickness in a hurry. We'd be sleeping in the those hammocks, then that ship would start rocking, then your feet would hit the deck and you'd go straight to the head, because you were going to lose it."

Other than the initial shock to his equilibrium, Milam's mining skills were in balance with what the Navy was seeking. "I could do just about anything they wanted done. I had plenty of experience in dynamite and black powder explosives from my work in the mines. So when I came in the Navy they tried to get me into the UDT (Underwater Demolition Team) group, and I told them, 'No, I'm not cut out for that.' Instead he went in as one of the hard working deck hands and a gunner.

Milam's first trip across the still-peaceful Pacific in mid-1941 was on the heavy cruiser *U.S.S. Louisville*. At that time most ships had no radar to detect the Japanese fleet expanding across the South Pacific. "The first radar we saw was when we were sitting in Pearl Harbor. We saw this ship that came in and it looked like it had a bed spring up on the mast, and we wondered what in the world that was. We asked somebody why a bed spring was attached to that ship. And he told us it was a radar, that it just came over from England, and that all the ships were going to get one. At that time we didn't know how important that thing would become." In fact, it was the joint British-American invention of radar that would begin to turn the tide of the war, first in the Atlantic, and eventually in the Pacific.

"During the time we had no radar we had to use human eyes, so you had to have some good lookouts. You were constantly scanning. When you're looking out, you don't just stare out. You keep looking side to side, because you can see more out of the side of your eyes than you can straight on. Once I learned how to do it, I was a pretty good spotter."

By late 1941 Milam could also spot that tensions were brewing between the United States and Japan. "We had been escorting ships out of China and running around out there in the Pacific, and we'd see a ship and zip!, it'd go the other way, really quick. And one day I was on the bridge and I said, 'Captain, you know that ship I reported about an hour ago, it's completely gone, he's really putting on the speed.' He said, 'Yeah, Japan's got ships all over the place out here.' We didn't even know how totally outgunned we were in everything until we got a radar and could spot all the stuff they had out there."

Despite deficiencies in armament and numbers, Milam says that the men in the Navy at that time were a "different breed of man." They were well-trained and had been hardened by the depression. "We were the best. If you didn't believe it, they'd tell you! Oh, there were some that were worried about what would happen with Japan, but I told them I wasn't going to worry about anything that might happen with them because I had already been through worse stuff than that could ever be. So someone asked me what would I do if a torpedo hit the ship. I told them I could swim. Then he said, 'Do you see any land around here?' That got me to thinking a little bit."

On December 6, 1941, vessels from the Pacific and Asiatic Fleets were in Manila, Philippines. Milam was one of the hundreds of men who left their ships to go on liberty that night in downtown Manila. "Me and a buddy of mine from the *Houston* went down to have a few drinks at the Silver Dollar Saloon. If you could drink five Singapore Slings and walk to the door without falling, you didn't have to pay for it. I never did make it to the door.

"Now back then, when liberty was up, the shore patrol would go around to all the bars and pick everybody up and put them back on their ships, and that's how I got back to my ship. When I woke up, I realized we were underway, and I knew we were underway at a high speed. So I asked, 'Where are we going?' They said the war had started, that Pearl Harbor had been bombed. We felt lucky we weren't at Pearl because we had been anchored right across from where the battleships were beaten up. We would have been right in the open, and probably would have been a good target." Tragically for Milam's friend on the *Houston*, the Japanese sank her several weeks after she left Manila. His friend, along with approximately 600 others on the ship, died.

Milam's ship, the *Louisville*, was ordered to complete her mission of escorting two ships back to the States. Before reaching stateside, they stopped at Pearl Harbor and were shocked at what they saw. "When we got in there we couldn't believe the devastation that was there. There were fires still burning all over everything, and the stink of the black oil, it had a terrible odor. We never dreamed it would be like that. When we left there months before, it was perfect looking, a quiet place that was clean as a whistle." Milam would later serve with some of the men who were on the bombed ships from Pearl. "When the battle horn went off, man, they were gone topside, right now! We asked them what they were in such a big hurry for. They told us they didn't want to be caught down below again. Then we started to figure out that those guys knew more than we did."

After coming back to the States briefly, Milam was transferred to a newly christened battleship, the *U.S.S. Indiana* (built in Newport News, the plank is now displayed at Nauticus). Despite the chance to serve on a new, modern battleship, Milam initially balked at the idea of leaving the *Louisville*. "I had been told by old sailors that your first ship is your favorite. It's just like your first girlfriend. I never ran into another ship that I liked as well."

Milam was part of the crew for the *Indiana's* shakedown cruise off the coast of Maine. He recalls, "During the shakedown, they fired all nine of the guns at one time, and rivets were flying out of the air ducts and everywhere else. We thought it was shrapnel, that somebody was shooting at us. They do that on a new ship to find out what happens so they have some idea what would happen during battle. That let me know this wasn't going to be an easy ride."

One of Milam's first wartime missions was to drop off marines for training for Guadalcanal. "Later on, when I was on an LST (Landing Ship Tank), we went into Guadalcanal and picked them up. They weren't the same people we had dropped off. I saw a lot of young boys go in there and come out old, deadly men. There was a young boy that looked like he wasn't more than ten or twelve years old when we took him in. But when we picked him up, he just sat there sharpening his knife, all the time, and he had the most deadly eyes I ever saw. I didn't realize until the latter part of the war how lucky I was to be on a ship."

Milam's closest encounter with the Japanese came while on the *Indiana*. "A destroyer had picked up some Japanese prisoners somewhere, and they were sending them over to us while we were at sea. So, we had to highline them over. I was running the line on the winch, and this lieutenant came over and said, 'You don't get one drop of water on these people. You understand that? If you do, you're going to be court-martialed.' No way in the world could we ever mistreat a prisoner, even though they mistreated our prisoners. That was tough, because they were cruel. Very cruel."

After his time on the *Indiana* Milam served shore duty at American Samoa. Eager to get back to sea, Milam was able to talk himself onto an LST. LSTs didn't have the appeal of the sleeker fighting ships, but they were the workhorses of the Navy.

Now back at sea, where he felt comfortable, Milam saw the Pacific from one end to the other. He jokes, "I think I was on every island there was in the Pacific." He went through New Georgia, Marcus Island, the Gilbert Islands, the Marshall Islands, Tarawa, Borneo, Tarakan, Guadalcanal, and the Mariana Islands.

Most of his stops took place after the islands had been secured, except for once. "We were picking up some Marines at Tarawa. There were still American bodies floating in the surf when we pulled in there. And you could see Japanese body parts amongst the coconut trees from the shore bombardment. They cut that island all to pieces. I don't think I saw but one or two coconut trees that were standing. Anyhow, I was on the bow looking down on the opening of the bow doors and watching the ramp come down so that the Marines could get on board, and there were gun bullets hitting in front of the ramp." It's one of the few times Milam admits to being scared while in the Pacific.

The other times were caused by torpedoes. More than once, lookouts perched high above in the ship's crows-nest spotted the telling white streak of an incoming torpedo. "I'll tell you, it's frightening when you see those streaks in the water. That's where it comes down to the captain knowing his ship and how to maneuver it to get out of the way. We had some good skippers. But those subs never did come up or we would've blown them out of the water. All they had to do was just show a periscope and we could pinpoint that thing."

Kamikazes were a different story. "A plane would have to have been pretty darn close for us to reach him with the small stuff we had on that LST. The old man called general quarters one time and I was thinking that I hoped to hell he didn't call for us to open fire. The pilot was too far up, but he could drop a hundred- pound bomb and that would have wiped us out right then. Sure enough, the old man passed the word over the phones, 'Open fire!' I told him that we didn't have anything to reach that man with. He asked me after the raid why I was afraid, and I told him that opening fire would aggravate him and all he was out there for was to be a nuisance."

Torpedoes and kamikazes aside, Milam's days in the Pacific were typical of what most sailors experienced during the war: monotonous tasks and endless anticipation. Day to day life was spent cleaning, training, or simply waiting for something to happen. "First thing in the morning, usually around six, there would be revelry. To keep everybody from running into each other, we had what we called traffic situations. You went up on the starboard side of the steps, and down on the port side. Then the next call would be for chow. And you had better know your calls." Despite the bad reputation that the infantry's K-rations and C-rations received, Milam smiles when he thinks back on chow time. "We were fed good. We had our own bakery on the ship. Those guys could flat out do some baking. Most times we had plenty of time to eat. But sometimes you might get interrupted half a dozen times with general quarters. You had to pay attention to that no matter what you were doing.

"We spent most of our time doing drills and taking care of the ship, keeping it clean. Everyday. You could eat off the decks, they were that clean. We had these white teak decks and every week we had to clean them. You'd get a whole line of men, and you had this brick-like brush that had a hole for a scrub brush handle. We'd scrub it with salt water, soap and sand. All that cleaning wasn't just for looks, it was primarily for infection control. One time we had six hundred to seven hundred men that were sick, and that'll practically stop a ship. Early on I always wondered why in the world they were so interested in keeping things so clean. I just knew that all we were going to do is to get it shot up. Then I started to realize it was to keep down any spread of infection.

"And you had to take a shower every night. Yes sir. We had people that would come into the Navy who had never done that before. You can't imagine how some people lived before they joined up. So we had sand and canvas that they'd use on people's bare skin if they wouldn't take a bath. Also, you had to shave every morning and every evening. You didn't want any beard. If you were going on watch, you had to look just like you were going to Sunday School."

But in Sunday School they didn't teach you how to keep your ship running when you're hundreds of miles from the nearest port. As the leading boatswains mate, Milam was responsible for getting his crew's hard-to-get supplies, regardless of how he did it. "We had to steal in order to operate the ship, because you got nothing. During the war, they just didn't give you enough. We were given very little money for our quarterly allotment. Out of that, I had to buy all the paint, all the cleaning gear, and all the tools. So I used the salvage yards at some of the islands. That's how it worked for getting supplies. The old man was scared to death because he knew we were stealing this stuff. He'd say, 'Don't tell me anything. I don't want to know.'

"And I could always get coffee and stuff from the mess (kitchen) and then go over to the gunners mates and get boxes of twenty-two shells for trading. Oh, those shells were good trading materials for stuff we needed. Once you knew how to work the system, then you'd have no problems. The thing was, you get on these ships that might be in the backwaters expecting to be gone for a month, but you end up out there for six. Well, you had to feed your crew and keep your ship clean, plus oil and tools and spare parts. If you didn't have some good thieves on there, you were going to miss out!

"An example is that we would go into these islands to pick up Marines and Seabees. We went into the Ellis Islands to pick up some Seabees once. Those guys had everything in the world there, stuff we had never seen, like coffee makers. They lived like kings. They even had inner-spring mattresses! And beer! So we eyeballed all this as they were bringing it on board, and ended up stealing quite a bit of it. Oh my, I tell you, we stole cases and cases of beer.

"One of the items we took was one of their big welding machines. A great big thing. I had the shipfitters build me a rack and set it up above a door, then we painted it navy blue and put a number on it. And then on the tank deck, there were these oval covers that were bolted down, and underneath it was a tank that we'd fill full of water. So we unbolted the covers and hanged stuff underneath the plates. That's where we put the short-wave radios we took.

"Well, it ended up that they brought in the Marine and Navy investigators to try to find that stuff. They went all through that ship. I mean they went through it. That welder was sitting in the most obvious place over a door, and the only thing they found was one can of beer! So we came back to that island again, it must have been six months later, and some of those investigators came on board again. As soon as they saw me, they said, 'We're not investigating this time, but we want to know how in the world did you people hide all that stuff you got? And especially that welder?' So I told them where we had hidden everything, and he said, 'I knew you people had stolen it right from under us! We even had some of our best investigators on that.'"

Other investigations would follow, not about stealing, but about crew members buying and selling items on the black market. The black market exploded in both the Pacific and Atlantic as a way for servicemen and civilians to get hard-to-find items. "I had heard of what some of the guys were doing, but I never did play around in it. I had enough sense to know that when you got in the black market, you were getting into some deep, deep waters."

Shortly before the war in the Pacific was over, Milam was sent back home because he "had been in the Pacific too long." But shortly after returning he was dispatched to San Juan, Puerto Rico, to operate a Navy tug-boat. Much of his job was spent towing out the anti-submarine nets around Puerto Rico. The nets were used to block German U-boats. Later promoted to chief, he ran one of the few crews in the Navy that was half white, half black. "We never had any problems. We lived together, even fought together when we'd go into San Juan and get into bar fights."

Eventually, Milam made another trip across the Pacific as part of the U.S. occupation force after Japan's surrender. It's from his time there that he has one of his favorite stories to tell. "One day Mrs. Gen. MacArthur came down to the ship with a sergeant that had escorted her. He came on board and was standing there and didn't know anybody. So I walked over and asked him if he had ever been on one of these things. He said no, so I said, 'I'll tell you what, we're going to have lunch pretty soon, so let's go take a tour of the ship and then we'll go down and have a good meal.' After that, when he got ready to leave, he asked me if I had ever been to Tokyo. I hadn't, so he told me he'd send a car for me to take me on the tour.

"So days later, word came down for me to report up to the quarterdeck immediately. I wondered what in the world I had done, and then I knew what it was for. So I rushed up there, and sure enough, another sergeant was standing there stiff as a board. And the officer of the deck said, 'This man's looking for you, and he says he's going to take you to the embassy. Who do you know up there?' And I said, 'Gen. MacArthur', and we took off. So we went right into the embassy, and MacArthur and his family were eating right there in the back."

Among the veterans with whom I've spoken, some have not had kind words for Douglas MacArthur. Milam is not one of them. "I always thought he was a pretty good leader. I think the reason some people didn't like him was military jealousy. Politics were vicious. The people who really knew him and worked with him, you very seldom ever heard them make a derogatory remark about him."

Regardless of what some may say about the man now, the Japanese people in 1945 showed MacArthur their full respect. Says Milam, "When he would leave the embassy in his motorcade, everything stopped. It's hard to imagine a city like that stopped with so many people. There was nothing moving. When he came through they bowed just like he was the emperor. And he knew it would be a good idea to have the Japanese as an ally. He was far-seeing on that."

As hordes of American servicemen continued to stream back across the Pacific to be discharged, Milam stayed put. He spent much of the next fifteen years as a chief at different stations in the Pacific. On some islands, even a decade after the war had ended, there were pockets of Japanese soldiers that still believed the war had not ended. "When we were on Guam there were Japanese in caves on the island. This was in '57, '58 and '59. They'd come out and steal clothes off the clothes line. We never did know how many there were, but they were just trying to survive. People would go up there and try to entice them out, but they didn't believe the war was over. See, they were brainwashed that nothing was going to happen. Japan was going to rule the whole world as far as they were concerned. But Truman dropped the atomic bomb and made a believer out of them."

After twenty-two years of living the life of a sailor, Milam retired in 1962. From breathing coal dust in West Virginia to breathing salt air in the Pacific, he has endless stories that are often told with a quick, sharp laugh. He is one of the old salts who hated war but loved the Navy. Now, at eighty years old, he and his wife of fifty-three years like to talk of how lucky they have been. As his wife says, "We've had a good life. Fifty-three years and I wouldn't trade any of them."

After being the man who got things done on his ships, he has now become the man that neighbors turn to for getting things fixed. From lawn mowers to fishing poles, he is Mr. Fixit. One also gets the impression that nearly every-one on his street knows who Leo Milam is. And that's the story of many of our World War II veterans. Long ago they were the backbone of the world's fight for democracy. Now, they're the neighbors who live as the backbone of our communities.

1942                                          2001

Buried in the myriad of our country's patriotic slogans during the war years was a motto coined by the Pittsburgh Courier, an influential black newspaper. Its "Double V" campaign stood for "Victory over fascism abroad, victory over racism at home." It was a statement, and a hope, in which a young man from Bertie County, North Carolina, would play a part.

Eldern Holley's great grandfather was a slave in Colerain, North Carolina. Eventually freed by Abraham Lincoln's Emancipation Proclamation, he went to work for a widow who promised him a slice of her sprawling farm. That slice ended up being 300 acres and that's where Eldern Holley would eventually grow up.

Born in 1920, Eldern entered the world as a part of the segregated South. It was a time when "coloreds" were required to drink from separate water fountains, get off the sidewalk if a white person approached, ride in the back of the bus, go to segregated schools and movie theaters, and the shameful list goes on and on.

But despite the blatant racism, Eldern recalls things as being pretty good back then, at least for him. "In those days, we were lucky. We had a place to stay and something to eat. See, we had those 300 acres. For blacks that was kind of unusual. And we had a good relation with the whites. When it came to tobacco farming, we would help them and they would help us. We needed one another because we were neighbors. The racial thing, I really didn't get much of that.

So when I got into the military, that affected me because I had always had good relations with the whites. Now a lot of the blacks, from north and south, hated the whites. Not me."

After finishing high school in 1939, Holley moved to Norfolk to join his brother and sister who had already moved there. His stay in Norfolk was short because by November 1941 his draft notice came. He was one of the first blacks drafted for service for World War II.

The history of blacks in the United States military is both a disgraceful and a proud one. Disgraceful because of how blacks were treated, proud because of their willingness and sacrifice despite that treatment. Their fight for America started early. One of the first men to die in the Revolutionary War was Crispus Attucks, a black man. Eventually, and quite ironically, over four thousand blacks, many of whom were slaves fought in America's quest for independence.

After fighting in the War of 1812, blacks were called upon again to fight for a nation that continued to treat them as second class citizens. Holding the hope of complete freedom, the Civil War employed nearly 400,000 men of African descent. While twenty black soldiers were awarded the Congressional Medal of Honor during the war, their participation was largely resented, and their desires were widely suspicious.

By World War I another 400,000 blacks were conscripted into the nation's white military. Although expected to fight in the same bloody trenches as the white doughboys, they would not do so side by side. In fact, segregation extended from training to transport to trenches.

Little would change in the years between the world wars. Discrimination and segregation were the accepted ways of military life. Despite their history of exemplary military service, blacks were thought to make only mediocre soldiers, perform well only under whites, and take longer to train. Such was the mindset of a time not that long ago.

At the start of World War II only about 4,000 black men were in America's armed forces. By the end of the war more than a million black men, and women, served. Serving in all theaters of the war, they fought against countries that often gave them more respect than did their own country. When they returned to the home for which they had risked their lives, they found the same racism and restraints that were there when they left.

It wasn't until 1943 that large numbers of the country's black population were called upon to fight and die overseas. That makes Eldern Holley's 1941 draft notice an unusual memento. "I was nervous, like anybody else," jokes Holley. "I didn't know anything about it. But the best training for a soldier is being a farmer. You have a lot of digging, there's a lot of work, you have to improvise, and you have long hours. As a farmer, I was used to all of that. So I had an advantage over a lot of the other kids that were in my unit."

As was blind tradition, Holley was sent to an all-black unit. Furthering that tradition was the fact that an overwhelming number of blacks in the military were used simply as slave labor. They drove the trucks, piloted the ferries, served the food, and cleaned the head. Remember, they weren't thought to make good soldiers. "Being from the South, I didn't know any better. At first they were hesitant about bringing the blacks into the service because they figured we'd want too many rights. But it was the white women (led by Eleanor Roosevelt) that really pushed for us to be in. And once we got in they realized we could fight like anybody else."

Holley would get a chance to prove himself in combat before most blacks. After going through his segregated boot camp at Fort Eustis, Virginia, he was assigned to an artillery unit that was sent overseas to fight in late 1942. He almost didn't make it there. While en route to their training facility near New Caledonia in the Pacific, Holley's ship, which was also segregated, hit a mine. As the ship floundered, then began to sink, the order was given to abandon ship. Holley was one of the last to jump.

Of the 6,000 on board, 50 died. After a brief 45 minutes in the water, rescue crews gathered the white and black soldiers from the oily water. "One funny thing about that is after swimming in that oil from the ship everybody was black!"

But the homogenous-looking ranks didn't last but a few hours. Once on shore, the troops rejoined their respective units to begin training for their assault on Bougainville, the last of the enemy-held Solomon Islands. It was a hot, steaming jungle that was the last gate to be opened before hitting the Philippines. It also hid over 25,000 Japanese soldiers.

In November of 1943, American Marines and Army infantry units invaded Bougainville. Following them was Holley's 54th Coastal Artillery unit. "Oh, that was hot. We were like a ten-cent piece on a paper dollar. Up in the mountains were Japanese. To your right was Japanese, and then some to your left. It was miserable. But being a country boy, I could take it."

Learning bloody lessons from Guadalcanal and New Georgia, the American plan was to take and protect only a small corner of the island, just big enough to build an airstrip. Instead of hunting the Japanese in the jungle, they would wait for the Japanese to come to them.

Holley's gun crew was in charge of a big 155 mm gun. It took twenty-two men to handle and fire the 110- pound shells. Dug in near the coast, they fired at targets that were called in from spotters. Since many of their targets were as much as 12,000 yards away, they never saw what they hit. "After we'd fire, the infantry would go in. One time, so I was told, the infantry went in and they found the Japanese crew dead, standing up. They were killed from the concussion of our shell."

The Japanese attacks on the tiny, yet well-defended American garrison were brutal and unrelenting. "Those big guns we had were about fifty meters apart, and many nights we got shells coming in between them. But we would dig down into the ground and put up logs and sandbags, so they had to have a direct hit to get you.

"We were right across the way from some Seabees (Navy engineers) and the Japanese came in one night and killed six of them. Just slit their throats. The Japanese were vicious. But that's how they were trained. So we were always on alert. From sunrise to sunset we never stood up. Everything you did you did it on your stomach or your back. When you needed to be relieved you tapped the guy next to you three times.

"I was told to go and get some sleep once. By the time I got to my tent, I heard them calling for a firing mission, and by their voice I knew it was hot. So I ran back to my gun, threw my headsets on, and by the time I had taken over, a shell hit my tent. I didn't have a toothbrush left. Just a big hole. It was a matter of only a few minutes.

"Since we were in artillery, we stayed put. But once we were in this spot which was kind of swampy, and there were these big trees maybe four to five feet in diameter with the roots on top of the ground. Well, when the Japanese would start shooting, the trees would start falling. I had one guy who was on another gun, and I knew the guy was nervous. He started running when the shells started coming in, and I ran behind him for about fifty meters to tell him to stop, but he was running like a deer. This tree fell, hit him right in the back and killed him. I tried to save his life but I just couldn't do it."

During the fighting at Bougainville, the relatively few black troops there fought in a separate sector from the rest of the troops. But, Holley says, as he repeated to me time and time again, neither he nor any of the other blacks were hassled or shunned by any white soldiers. It's a sentiment that seems to fly in the face of how our black troops were treated back home. "For me, I always felt that if I treated people right they were going to treat me right. Plus, I was young, I was strong, I did my job well, and I had a lot of confidence in myself."

By March of 1944, four months after U.S. forces landed, the fighting on Bougainville was coming to a close. Yet Holley was stationed there a full year. While there, he was promoted to corporal and placed in charge of his gun crew. Two weeks after that, he was promoted to sargeant due to his exemplary work with his crew. "If you could perform and do your job, the promotions came pretty fast."

With the push towards Tokyo rolling northward, Holley's unit was sent to New Guinea, then to the Philippines to prepare for the invasion of Japan. While there he was again promoted, this time to first sargeant major and placed in charge of approximately 175 men, all black. "We were scheduled to go to Japan from the Philippines. I was on a ship headed closer to Tokyo Bay when I got word that they had dropped the A bomb. The thing about that bomb is that it's sad it killed so many Japanese, but we saved a lot of Americans. But really, they asked for it, and that bomb may have saved my life."

Holley thought the bomb also meant an end to his Army days. With his mission scrubbed, Holley was back in the States by December 1945. "I went in to get processed out. As I went in, I said my name, and this sergeant major says, 'Are you First Sgt. Holley?' I told him yes. He asked me, 'Are you getting out?' I again told him yes. He said, 'Son, if you made first sargeant in just four years then you've got something the Army needs. Now I suggest you stay in, and we'll send you anywhere you want to go, and we'll give you a vacation.' So I decided it would be a good thing for me to do. I got ninety days vacation in North Carolina and I picked Germany to be stationed just because I had never been there."

By 1948 President Truman did what should have been done decades before. He integrated the military. Part of that integration meant black soldiers would officially lead white soldiers for the first time in United States military history. One of the first black men to do that was Eldern Holley. Selected from a field of twenty other first sergeants, he was assigned to a transport unit in Germany. "One day a general came down and he wanted to see me in private, so we went in to the cafeteria to have a cup of coffee. He said, 'So, how do you treat the white soldiers?' I told him, 'Like soldiers.'"

Some of the other black soldiers didn't quite see things that simply. "After my first tour in Germany, I was stationed in Kansas. As first sargeant I was on the board for promotions. One time we had something like three promotions and they were all white. So the blacks kind of complained about it to me. I said, 'Listen, you need to get a book, go to school, get some classes, go to the library or whatever and improve your education. That's your problem.' And over the years, blacks started getting those promotions. But I wasn't going to promote somebody that wasn't qualified. The blacks thought I was letting the brothers down, but I figured I was doing the right thing. The whites were just more qualified, so that's who I promoted. There were no quotas. You had to be qualified to be able to get the job."

During his second three-year tour in Germany, Holley's star continued to rise. His name was submitted to the Pentagon for a promotion to command sergeant major. His record of service, his fairness, his commitment to the Army, assured him of the promotion.

It also assured him of more overseas duty. After a year in Korea in the early 1960s, Holley was sent to Vietnam in 1969. While there, his helicopter was shot down...twice. Surviving both crashes, he also escaped North Vietnamese attacks on his units. Once again, as he had done more than twenty years earlier, Holley saw many of America's youth die. The difference in Vietnam, he says, is that it was a mistake. "In World War II, we had to be there. But in Vietnam, we had no business being there. No business at all. I remember looking in a tent once where some young boys had been killed and just thinking what a waste."

In 1973, after 34 years of military service, Holley retired. It was a long, victorious road for a country kid from the once-segregated farming towns of North Carolina. He says the military has come just as far as he has. "Between then and now is like night and day. Now, the most integrated part of our society is the military. That racial thing, we couldn't fix that overnight. I knew it was going to take some time to do it. But you teach a guy how to shoot guns, how to shoot missiles, and then tell him he's not a citizen? It doesn't work that way."

Displayed in Eldern Holley's home in Virginia Beach, where he has lived for the past 33 years, and also just a few blocks from where I grew up, is a large portrait of him in his dress uniform. What you notice about the picture is not the color of the man's skin. What you see, what comes across, as you look at the medals beneath his confident visage, is a man proud of the country he served, proud of the obstacles he overcame, and proud of what has happened since. He fought for our country not as a black man, but simply as an American.

1943

2001

He was born, raised, and has since lived almost his entire life within one quarter of a mile from where he lives now. It's because of those deep roots to his home in southern Chesapeake that I first met Horace Curling. One Sunday morning I saw his name attached to an editorial in *The Virginian-Pilot*. He was complaining about the increased jet noise at Fentress Airfield, adjacent to his rural home. In that editorial he also mentioned he was a veteran of World War II, having fought in Italy, France, and Germany. Hoping he would be as vocal about his war years as he was about the jet noise, I gave him a call.

Curling attended Great Bridge High School, as did my mother, and graduated in 1941. At that time, young men were required to register for the draft when they turned 18. But it was two years before his number was called. "I was driving trucks for Berkley Feed Corporation, and there were three of us drivers that were drafted into the Army on the same day," he laughs. His feelings about it weren't very lighthearted back then. "Naturally, you are afraid of the unknown because you don't know what's going to happen to you. And you feel pretty sure that you're going overseas and you don't know if you're ever coming back. There's a lot of anxiety." Adding to the anxiety was that he would be leaving behind his bed-ridden mother. Her care would be left to Curling's two sisters.

"When I was 'invited' by Uncle Sam to join the Army, I rode a train for the first time when I left Portsmouth. That's where the draft board was. The train carried you to Richmond to be examined. As you went in, they'd tell you to pull off all your clothes, leave them on the floor, and then you walked around naked all day going from station to station. They were all Army officers checking us out. At one station they'd listen to your heart, another they'd examine your eyes. I used to say that they just counted your eyes and made sure you had a heart! That was about it for the examination. When you finished, you put your clothes on and they called your name. If you passed you went to one side of the room, if you failed you went to the other side. There were very few failures. Most everybody went. Then they made you take the oath and swore you in right then. Then they let you come home to straighten out all your affairs for seven days. At the end of those seven days, you reported back to the draft board."

After their brief break before basic training, the local Army recruits were sent to Camp Lee, now Fort Lee, just outside of Petersburg. The first non-commissioned officer Curling met after getting off the train was a former heavyweight boxer, Billy Conn. Conn was a bit of a celebrity since he had just fought Joe Louis earlier that year. "Conn was really a nice person, for how famous he was," nods Curling. His other memory of Camp Lee is pulling KP duty his second night there and having to peel potatoes all night long.

From there, the train trip got much longer. He took a troop train that zigzagged across the eastern U.S., picking up new troops. They were to spend the next thirteen weeks at basic training in Arkansas, where Curling would get an unexpected opportunity. "I had hurt my ankle playing football at Great Bridge High School my senior year. And if I did a whole lot of walking it would swell. Now there were a lot of people trying to get out of marches, and that's what they thought I was doing when I told them about my ankle. But towards the end of our thirteen weeks, we had to make thirty-mile hikes. And at the end of one of those thirty-mile trips, the medic had to cut my shoe off my foot because my foot was swollen so bad. That was the end of my marching days."

That was also the end of his days in Arkansas. While the rest of his buddies were sent immediately to the Pacific, he was sent to Fort Bragg, North Carolina, for field artillery training. He was trained on an eight-inch howitzer, which took a crew of twenty-four men to fire the two-hundred-pound shells. "I was the gunner, so I was the one who aimed the gun according to the directions given by headquarters. My position was on the left side of the gun, and that is why my hearing is so bad in my right ear. And the concussion was so great that if you didn't have your pants legs tucked into your boots, it would split your pants legs up to your knee."

While at Fort Bragg, Curling also had a chance to meet one of the war's most famous pinup girls, Betty Grable. "While we were stationed there, she actually ate lunch at our table. She looked better than she did in the movies!"

By August of 1943, he watched the Statue of Liberty fade from sight as he left America in a convoy of one hundred ships headed for Europe. To get there, the convoy went south to Florida, and then planned to turn into the Atlantic. "That first night, they cut all the engines on the ships and just floated off the coast of Florida. They had spotted some German subs. So, the Navy cruisers and destroyers went around dropping depth charges. The next morning, when we resumed our trip, they informed us over the public address system that six German subs had been sunk off the coast of Florida. The rest of the trip was pretty uneventful."

The convoy eventually landed at Oran in North Africa, but spent only a few weeks there. The Germans had but a few pockets of resistance left in North Africa, so Curling's division was only called upon to fire its gun a few times. Regardless, his time there would be long enough to get court-martialed. "We had our guns in position, and we were cleaning and oiling them. General Patton and a couple of aides just happened to drive by and saw us without shirts on. So he drove up there and had everyone of us court-martialed for going without a shirt. They took two-thirds of one month's pay! That was the fine (Curling received $68 per month as a corporal). Then the next day, Patton turned around and issued an order that you could go without a shirt. That was the kind of guy he was. The men hated him."

Curling also has an odd recollection from North Africa about mattress covers. "Everyone was issued a mattress cover. It was to be your body bag if you were killed. Almost everyone traded them to the Arabs for something to drink. The Arabs would then cut a hole in the bag for their head, and two arm holes and wear them for clothes."

Before leaving North Africa, Curling had a chance to catch one of Bob Hope's USO shows...almost. "The night he was supposed to put on his show, the Germans dive-bombed and strafed the area and there were quite a few casualties. So instead of him putting on a regular show, he and the group he was with had to just walk around and talk with you, light your cigarette, and tell a little joke trying to cheer you up."

After Oran, thousands of men were gathered in the Mediterranean for the assault on Sicily and Italy. It was still too early in the planning and training stages for the invasion of France, but Sicily and Italy were attractive alternatives. The Allies wanted to tie up as many German resources as possible in Italy in order to keep them away from France and the Eastern Front. Winston Churchill referred to this plan as striking at the "soft underbelly" of Germany. Sicily was first and was secured by August of 1943. What would soon be called the "Bloody Boot" of Italy was next.

Salerno, Italy, was the jumping-off point for the invasion of Europe. The assault began in September of 1943 and Horace Curling was a part of it. The fighting was initially heavy. German counterattacks threatened to push the

American and British forces back. Fortunately for Curling and the rest of his heavy artillery division, they arrived three days after the initial landing. The beachhead was secure by then, but he says they were still "greeted rather rudely by the Germans."

"We actually landed in a section that was being held by the British. I was glad to leave them because those people would stop right in the middle of a battle and build a big fire and brew a pot of tea! Shells were falling all around everything and they'd be there eating. In fact, when we were in North Africa, we replaced a British division. And I heard it told that the British and Germans would fight up to about five in the afternoon, and they'd call a truce. Then they'd go into some little town and drink wine. The British troops would be on one side of a tavern, the Germans on the other. Then they got back out there the next morning and started fighting again."

The fighting in Salerno lasted only a few weeks, but the grizzly grind up the Bloody Boot was just beginning. Allied troops faced the daunting task of moving northward to their primary prize of Rome. They would be forced to fight not only against the Germans, but against an unrelenting rainy season, scores of mountains and rivers, and the narrow shape of Italy, which favored the German defensive positions. Curling thinks about this and says, "That was where we really found out what war was all about."

The Allied advance was halted seventy-five miles south of Rome. It was there that the Allies suffered through a long, wet winter. "In Italy," Curling says flatly, "they have a six-month rainy season and I think it rained every day of those six months. Back then, you didn't have rain shoes or sleeping bags or anything. You had wool blankets, regular boots, and we might have had a raincoat. We did have long underwear, but we weren't equipped very well. To sleep, you would dig a foxhole in a ditch bank. But it was so rainy, sometimes you'd go to get in your foxhole to go to sleep and before morning your blanket would be floating from all the rain."

All of that rain produced a morass of mud in which the men and machines were mired. The famed World War II cartoonist Bill Mauldin spent much of his overseas time in Italy. Curling actually saw him several times there. In his book *Up Front*, Mauldin suggested a way for the folks back home to have some idea of what living was like in the muddy mountains of Italy:

*"Dig a hole in your back yard while it is raining. Sit in the hole until the water climbs up around your ankles. Pour cold mud down your shirt collar. Sit there for forty-eight hours, and, so there is no danger of your dozing off, imagine that a guy is sneaking around waiting for a chance to club you on the head or set your house on fire.*

*"Get out of the hole, fill a suitcase full of rocks, pick it up, put a shotgun in your other hand, and walk on the muddiest road you can find. Fall flat on your face every few minutes as you imagine big meteors streaking down to sock you. After ten or twelve miles (remember - you are still carrying the shotgun and suitcase ) start*

*sneaking through the wet brush. Imagine that somebody has booby-trapped your route with rattlesnakes which will bite you if you step on them. Give some friend a rifle and have him blast in your direction once in a while.*

*"Snoop around until you find a bull. Try to figure out a way to sneak around him without letting him see you. When he does see you, run like hell all the way back to your hole in the back yard, drop your suitcase and shotgun, and get in.*

*"If you repeat this performance every three days for several months you may begin to understand why an infantryman sometimes gets out of breath. But you still won't understand how he feels when things get tough."*

Curling also laments about the Italian people whom he was there to liberate. "The Italians just resented us, it seemed like, even though we were saving their country. The German people treated us better than the Italian or French people ever did. Their country was torn up pretty bad, so that's one reason I guess. They'd try to cheat you out of everything. If you tried to buy a bottle of wine, sometimes it wouldn't be wine at all. It'd be a bottle of muddy water, or something else. And they always wanted cigarettes and candy bars. One day we found this thirteen-year-old girl around our kitchen scratching through the garbage picking out something to eat. Supposedly both her parents had been killed. So our first sergeant, he was an elderly man of about sixty-years old, he took a liking to her because he said he had a grand daughter about the same age. He put her up in a tent, fed her, and let her work around the kitchen."

The next target on the road to Rome was the small, prewar resort town of Anzio, only thirty miles south of Rome. The landing took place behind enemy lines, completely surprising many of the German units. The initial surprise allowed the Americans to easily push three to four miles inland. But by the end of the day, thousands of Germans were rushing to Anzio and the Americans were forced to dig in. Hitler referred to it as the "Anzio abscess" and wanted it removed. What would follow would be four long months of constant bombing, shelling, and fighting, marking some of the most bitter fighting of World War II.

Anzio stands out as one of Curling's worst memories of the war. "The Germans could reach any spot on that beachhead with their artillery. That was rough. They could actually hit the ships bringing in supplies. One time, the Germans launched a counterattack and said they were going to push us back into the Mediterranean. We had to fire our gun for seventy-two hours straight. They weren't even bringing in any food to us. All they brought us was ammunition. Our little kitchen had coffee and these things we called hardtack biscuits. That's all we had for three days. We were the only heavy artillery battalion on the beachhead, so we were always busy defending our position and the other units there. Our gun position was right in the middle of an ammunition dump, which was a prime target for the Germans. That made it even more dangerous for us."

Despite the mounting casualties in deaths and wounded among the Americans, Curling's division was lucky. Only three were killed. One of those killed was within inches of Curling. "There were three of us standing side by side at our gun. A German shell landed near by, and the boy over on my left had a piece of shrapnel that went through his head and took the whole top part of his head off. He died instantly. That was the first guy I had seen killed. It'll really shake you up when you see something like that. You don't ever forget it, especially when it's one of your best buddies and he falls on your arm dead."

It was the constant shelling, with it's ripping, deadly shrapnel, that not only claimed many lives at Anzio, but also broke men mentally. "The German eighty-eight shells had holes drilled in them, so they made a loud whistle when they were coming down. That whistle would get so loud it seemed it was going to come down your shirt collar. We had a boy in our outfit from Georgia. He acted like a rough, tough guy. But whenever the Germans would start shelling, if those shells would land anywhere close around, he would get up in a corner of sandbags, and he would shake like a leaf on a tree. Ordinarily he didn't smoke, but during the shelling he might have two cigarettes going at the same time. It would unnerve him so much that he just couldn't handle it."

In 2001, there are still veterans of Anzio living in Hampton Roads. There are also the widows. I met with Jean Collins in her Virginia Beach home one afternoon as she showed me her husband's collection of photos and other memories from Anzio. Staff Sgt. Daniel Collins survived Anzio, made it back home, but passed away in 1996. He was awarded the bronze star at Anzio for his uncanny ability to deliver supplies to the front-line troops. "He couldn't drive a nail straight, but he could get those guys pretty much anything they needed," smiles Collins. Among the assortment of items she showed me was a poem.

> "...As our casualties mounted in this horrible war,
> How many we lost I kept no score,
> One thing for certain that I do know,
> There was no place like Anzio"

I asked Horace Curling what kept him going at Anzio. "Survival, I guess. I don't think anyone ever gets to the point of not being scared. I know I didn't." Just east of Anzio lies the Sicily-Rome Cemetery. Covering seventy-seven acres, the site is dedicated to the Americans killed there and in the surrounding towns. Dotting the immense field of dark green are the white headstones of 7,862 military dead.

After four months the Allies broke out of Anzio and the surrounding valleys and mountains and finally liberated Rome. It was there that Curling had a chance to watch the Pope deliver a sermon from a balcony at the Vatican.

At the other end of the celebrity spectrum, he also had a chance to meet country legend Grandpa Jones. "He put on a show while we were moving up through Italy. And after the show he gave us a ride back to our outfit in his Army vehicle. They even called him Grandpa back then and he was a young man." Curling also had the opportunity to see the Leaning Tower of Pisa as the troops pushed farther north into the Tuscany region.

After reaching the southern Alps many troops in Italy were pulled back to Naples to regroup for the invasion of southern France. The invasion took place at Marseilles shortly after the initial breach of Hitler's Atlantic Wall farther to the north in Normandy. "The invasion at Marseilles was a piece of cake," says Curling. "The Germans were concentrating all of their troops up in Normandy, so southern France was pretty easy."

Not only was the fighting easier, but the weather and accommodations were better. Instead of a cold, muddy foxhole, Curling was often afforded a night's stay in an abandoned farm house, or some type of shelter as the Army moved through a string of small villages. But it wasn't all easy. "We had put our kitchen in a two-story building in some small town. And one day, right about noon, a German plane came over and our antiaircraft were shooting at it. And I'm sure the German just kicked out the bomb in his haste to get away, but it actually went right through the roof of where our kitchen was. One of my buddies, he was from Norfolk, was killed, and there wasn't a scratch or mark on him anywhere. They said it had to be the concussion that did it.

"We spent our off time in the home of a French widow with two small children. Her food supply was very limited but she was always willing to share what she had. All of us would bring whatever we could get from our kitchen to her and the children. I remember her baking a birthday cake for one of us from what little supplies she had. She would wash our clothes and cook things for us. She was like a mother to all of us."

As Curling and the rest of the Allies approached the German border, the heavy fighting and its resultant number of wounded and dead began to climb again. Even so, Curling's thoughts on the Germans echo those of other veterans with whom I've spoken. "They were good soldiers, and they were good people. The German SS Troops, now they were the mean ones. But the regular German Army, they were just like us. They were drafted and put in the army. They didn't want to be there any more than we did."

Curling was fortunate to be part of a division blessed with relatively light fighting as they approached the Rhine and crossed into Germany. There was still tough fighting from time to time, and men continued to die, but his memories of the push to Berlin center more on German retreats and surrenders than on fighting. "Sometimes before we could get our gun up in position, they would already be out of range because they were retreating. So we had to move again. I remember one time I was driving the jeep for the captain and he was looking for a new position for our guns, so he was looking at the road map. We came to this crossroad and we stopped so he could figure out which way to go, and a German soldier raised up out of the brush, raised his hands and hollered, 'Comrade!' Our captain told him to get in the back of our jeep and we would take him back to a POW camp. And he said, 'No, No, No, me got field of Comrades!' I bet there were a hundred German soldiers just laying there hiding over there in the brush. The captain told them we couldn't handle all of them. So he told them to just line up and start marching toward the back. Some of them were old men, some of them were young. Some were wounded. They were hungry. But a lot of them were just happy then.

"We had four or five German prisoners that worked around our kitchen. We had a little house trailer that they slept in at night. We had to post a guard outside the trailer at night, but they weren't going anywhere. They had food and they were safe. One of them was an older fella and everybody called him Pop. He was a good baker. He'd get in the kitchen and bake up all kinds of cookies and bread. When the war ended, they were going to release him, let him go, but he didn't want to go. He said he didn't have anywhere to go. He didn't have a home or any family left. I don't know whatever happened to him."

Curling's division had made it to the Bavarian Mountains when Germany surrendered in May of 1945. He talks of how beautiful and picturesque the area was. It had been spared the devastation of Allied bombing since there were few industrial sites in the region. But soon after the war, the sight and smell of the Nazi's reign of terror was made clear to many American troops as they passed through the concentration camps.

"I didn't see any of it until after the war ended, " Curling says quietly. "But we did see several of the camps. They were some horrible looking places. They would dig these great big pits and put lyme in it. When the Jews and Russians and whomever would get so sick and diseased and couldn't work anymore, they threw their bodies in that lyme pit. The lyme would eat them up. And they had those great big ovens like you would use to bake bread. And they would put a live person and shove them up inside that oven. They had cleaned all that up with disinfectant by the time we got there."

After the war ended and the concentration units were liberated, many of the former Russian prisoners were out for revenge on the Germans. "The camps were out in the countryside where the German people were. These refugees would go to the Germans' houses and steal whatever they wanted. Take their food and kill their animals. So the U.S. Army started putting three or four soldiers at each little farm to protect the German people from the refugees. That's what I did for about three months after the war.

"The American kitchen would come around and bring you a meal once a day. But this farm where we were staying at, those people had plenty of food, and they fed us good." Curling comments that the American soldiers didn't mind their new role as protectors for the Germans. Instead, they thought of it as good duty compared to what they had just been through.

By September of 1945 Curling was finally on his way back home. By October he saw the landmark that he had seen two years and two months before: the Statue of Liberty. There was no ticker-tape parade to welcome back his troop ship, just the Red Cross and the Salvation Army. "One thing that still stands out in my mind was the Red Cross giving out coffee. But you had to buy the doughnuts that they offered. The Salvation Army was also there and everything they had was free. That is one reason I always try to support them to this day."

Curling was discharged from the Army in Maryland, then took a Trailways bus to Norfolk, where one of his sisters greeted him. That night, like so many other families across the country, the Curling family welcomed back their son, by then a man. "I think I had grown up a lot. I had a better understanding of getting along with people and of cooperation. When it came to the man next to you, you're depending on him, and he's depending on you in life-and-death circumstances." He still sends and receives Christmas cards and letters from some of those men he fought beside in Italy, France, and Germany.

At the urging of his children and grandchildren, Horace Curling began putting in writing his memories of the war. His hope is that his history will survive, in some small way, within them. He has a grandson attending West Point who continues to ask questions of his grandfather, wanting to know what the young men of another generation were asked to sacrifice. Hopefully Curling's grandson will never be asked to do the same.

# RONALD SPANGLER

1942

2001

The flames were still burning at Pearl Harbor when Ron Spangler marched into the Marine Corps recruiting station in Norfolk. He was only seventeen years old, but he knew that when he fought the Japanese he wanted to do it as a Marine. At that time, those who joined the Marines were thought to either be brave, crazy, or have something to prove. Spangler claims none of the above, simply saying, "I just saw a sign that said the Marines wanted good men, so I enlisted with them. I wanted to fight for my country. Patriotism, I guess."

The legend of the tough-guy, get-it-done, grit Marine was alive and well when Spangler joined in early 1942. Their recruitment standards were the highest and their boot camp was the toughest and longest. Strictly volunteer recruits, initially they faced three months of exhausting physical and mental training, not to mention the ticks, chiggers, mosquitoes, and snakes that awaited them on infamous Parris Island, South Carolina.

"It was kind of rough," Spangler says flatly. "One funny thing, though, is you got up at six in the morning and they immediately wanted you to go in and shave. One morning I was still standing by my bunk because I didn't need to shave. So the drill instructor says, 'Why aren't you shaving?!' I said, 'I'm not old enough to shave, Sir. No beard.' He said, 'If you're old enough to be a Marine, you're old enough to shave. Now get in there and shave!' So I'd just go in there and go through the motions."

Spangler made it through boot camp and was then sent to the Marine base at New River, North Carolina, for assignment to the 1st Marine Division. After being trained in antitank tactics, he spent thirty-one days riding a troop ship with 5,000 other boys-turned-men. They were headed across the Pacific to New Zealand to await orders on where and when they would face the Japanese. They were America's first counterpunch.

During the Marines three months in New Zealand, the United States had some big decisions to make. The Japanese were storming south through the Pacific quickly and held control of the air and sea. They were striking at will, taking what they wanted, and winning the war. The Japanese military's next step was to set up an airfield far enough south in the Solomon Islands to help them hit Australia effectively, and also help block the Americans from interfering. That airfield was to be at a little-known island named Guadalcanal.

The Americans were determined for that airfield at Guadalcanal to be built, but not by the Japanese. Yet in mid-1942, there was only one group trained and manned for an invasion. That was Spangler's 1st Marine Division. The Marine creed of "First to Fight" was about to be put to the test. The Battle of Midway and the Coral Sea had already taken place by August 1942, and the Japanese had been narrowly defeated. But those took place at sea. Americans at home waited anxiously to see how our boys stacked up, face to face, against a fighting machine that was on a rout. Guadalcanal was the ring for round one.

The division's officers were given thirty days to prepare for the invasion. The Marines were rushed to Fiji for training maneuvers, then loaded onto grimy, dank troop transports and sent to Guadalcanal by the first week of August.

Possibly realizing the significance of the task at hand, an officer addressed his Marines before the landings by saying, "We are fighting for a just cause, there is no doubt about that. It is for right and freedom. We have enjoyed the many advantages given to us under our form of government, and with the help of God, we will guarantee that same liberty and freedom for our loved ones and to the people of America for generations to come."

When the 1st Marine Division stormed ashore at Guadalcanal, nothing happened. "There wasn't any opposition at all on our landing," says Spangler. "The Japanese were building that airfield, so they did have a lot of construction people there, but when the Navy started bombing the island, they all left and went into the jungles. And they were even eating when they left, so food was still on their plates." The landings went so smoothly that the only casualty on August 7 was a Marine who cut himself trying to open a coconut. The relative quiet during those first few hours ended abruptly that afternoon.

The Japanese air and naval forces immediately converged upon Guadalcanal and the small island of Tulagi, where Marines had landed as well.

Shelling from ships and bombing by Bettys (term given to type of Japanese aircraft) rained down on the Marines. Although U.S. air and naval forces were effective initially, they became overwhelmed, were battered, and then were forced to retreat from the islands after only two days. When they left, so did the Marines' air and naval cover, as well as thousands of pounds of supplies, including food. One Marine later commented, "I know I had a feeling, and I think a lot of others felt the same way, that we'd never get off that island alive."

The weeks that followed were filled with Japanese bombing from the air and sea, as well as harrowing attacks on the ground. Japanese aircraft would come in groups each afternoon, then come again individually throughout each night, to bomb the defensive perimeter of the Marines. Spangler nods, "That was the worst thing, the bombing. You could be a mile from where it actually hit, but that thing would come screaming down, and you'd feel like it was going to land in the foxhole with you. They said that if you didn't hear it coming down, that was the end for you. Then the ships would come in there and shell, and we'd fire back, but we couldn't hit them because they were zigzagging. Later on, when they tried to retake the island, they shelled us all night so they could land more troops."

While digging in and preparing for the eventual ground counterattack, Spangler and the rest of the Marines also had to fight the steaming jungle. Martin Clemens, one of the coast watchers, described Guadalcanal as "beautiful...on the outside. On the inside she was a poisonous morass. Crocodiles hid in her creeks or patrolled her turgid backwaters. Her jungles were alive with slithering, crawling, scuttling things; with giant lizards that barked like dogs, with huge red furry spiders, with centipedes and leeches and scorpions, with rats and bats and fiddler crabs and a big species of land crab which moved through the bush with all the stealth of a steamroller."

And then there was the rain. "I think it rained the first month we were there," Spangler says. "It would rain all night, so you'd be laying in the mud. Mostly what we did was dig a foxhole about three to four feet deep and put a shelter half over top of us. But we still stayed wet."

Personal hygiene was another challenge. "I don't think I took many baths. You either had to go out in the ocean or into one of the rivers to get clean. And they wanted you to shave in case you got burned. And we didn't have any way to wash our clothes, so I ended up just throwing away my socks and underwear, and just went without them." Bathroom facilities were uncovered slit trenches.

In addition to the unending Japanese shelling and bombing, plus the lack of sleep, the rain, and the island's voracious creatures and mosquitoes, our troops were also weakened by limited food rations. Since the Navy, with much of the Marines' supplies still on board, had been forced to escape only two days after the landing, rations were quickly cut back to two meals a day.

"Most of what we had was C rations," Spangler recalls. "They were about the size of a can of pork and beans. They had either meat and beans, a vegetable stew, or a hash. It was pretty good, but we'd have the same thing every day. The meat and beans were the best, so everybody tried to get them. Mostly what we got was a sheep's tongue. It came from Australia and New Zealand. It was just a pickled sheep's tongue in a can. You were hungry, so you had to eat. It was sort of tough, and it still had some of the skin on it. But when you got hungry, you ate it. Then they brought in corned beef from Australia, too. And eventually we got B rations, which was cooked food." Among the few pleasant things the Marines found on the island were cases of beer the Japanese construction crews had left behind when they fled into the jungles. In addition to the beer, they also left an ice maker, which Spangler says made for a nice, cold beer.

Even though air and naval attacks quickly grew in ferocity, the airfield, named Henderson Field, was finished only a week after the landings. The airfield was a breath of life to the Marines. It made it possible for more planes (one of which was flown by Bert Earnest) to help protect the island, as well as serving as a vital supply vein. "When the B-17s finally made it in, the pilots would bring candy in a burlap bag and stand on the plane and dump it," Spangler chuckles. "All of us would dive in after it like a bunch of animals. But you know, it got to be so bad at that airfield at night from the Japanese shelling, that the pilots would come up to the front line and stay with us. It was safer to be there around our guns."

The real threat to our forces at Guadalcanal slowly took it's toll. Spangler may not have been on the front line, but the mosquitoes made no distinction between front-line flesh and that which was three to four hundred yards behind. "Oh, there were plenty of mosquitoes. Every kind imaginable. They could bite your foot and it'd swell up. They carried all kinds of diseases, like malaria. When we first landed they gave us shots of atabrine to suppress the symptoms of malaria in case you got it. But it made your eyes turn yellow, and you'd still get malaria. Early on, we had bug nets set up near the beach defense, and the colonel came around and looked at it and made us tear it all down. He said the Japanese would be able to see it from the air. So we were completely exposed. You can get used to living in just about any kind of conditions." But getting used to the malaria was a different story. Sickness caused by malaria would soon cause more U.S. casualties than the Japanese would. Some 5,601 Americans were stricken by its effects. Ron Spangler was one of them.

"I got it about a month after I was there. When I first got it, I'd get chills and start shaking all over, and then I'd get a fever of about 105. And then I got dysentery along with it. So they put me in the dispensary for a while, and when I was really bad off they kept me there. To treat it, they gave you quinine. It made your ears ring, and it made your heart beat fast. It was terrible stuff." Yet Spangler was still expected to, and still wanted to, stand his gun watches. Only when the infection became too overwhelming did he retreat to the dispensary. "But I would've rather been back with my outfit than sitting around in there. Mainly because you were sick anyway, and they'd keep you in those shelters for hours. And during the air raids, they'd just put you outside in a dugout. It was awful."

Spangler's malaria was to serve as his ticket off the island. "After I had been in the field hospital a while, I asked the doctor if I could go back to my outfit. He checked me over and told me I was dehydrating and that he was going to evacuate me out. I probably weighed 150 pounds when I got there, and weighed about 100 when they evacuated me. I felt sorry for my buddies that I was leaving behind, but I was glad to get away from there."

In the weeks before he made it out, the battle against the Japanese was beginning to escalate as thousands of their troops were pouring onto the island. While most of us consider the night a time for rest and sleep, it was anything but that for the Marines. "We did more sleeping in the daytime because they did a lot of their fighting at night, like at 3 A.M.," Spangler says with a frown. He also echoes a comment made by many U.S. troops that were on Guadalcanal by saying, "I used to hate it when it was pitch dark. But we always had ways to see the Japanese by using different kinds of flares. Our ships that came in would shoot in parachute flares all night long, or we'd have flares we'd shoot with the artillery. Plus, everyone would go down to the barbed wire and hang their ration cans on it. Then we'd have machine guns aiming at the wire, and if we heard any noise from those cans, we'd open up on them."

A September 1942 article in *The Washington Post* painted a grave picture for the folks at home. "News from the Solomons," said the *Post*, "is far from hopeful...it is ominous. Our forces may be dislodged from the precarious foothold they obtain on Guadalcanal." Spangler agrees with that tone by recalling, "We were told that if the Japanese landings were successful we probably couldn't hold the island. Those of us that were left were supposed to go up in the mountains and fight guerilla warfare. They figured they had us outnumbered five to one. I think we were able to hold them back by just good fighting techniques."

The techniques the Japanese used were considered by Americans as suicidal. By the hundreds, the Japanese hurled themselves at the Marines' defensive perimeter. Stories of these attacks are frightening and gruesome. They often involve heavily outnumbered Marines trying to hold back a swarm of screaming Japanese who would sometimes break through the perimeter and inflict death by use of either rifle, bayonet, or machete. Despite the fear these attacks caused, and the enormous odds against the Marines, Japanese losses were far higher than American. "The Japanese philosophy was to just charge.

So we'd kill five hundred of them with just twenty-five of our men. And you could see them coming and hear them yelling and hollering. It was really unbelievable what they would do," Spangler remembers as he shakes his head.

That's how it was for almost seven months. But with daily reinforcements of supplies and Army troops finally making it through, the Americans battled to win the war's first ground offensive.* And like the many other battles that would follow, victory would come at the cost of many lives. The Marines alone lost 621 in taking the island; another 1,517 Marines were wounded. An estimated 30,000 Japanese soldiers and sailors were killed.

By late 1943 Guadalcanal would serve as a temporary home for hundreds of thousands of American soldiers, sailors, and Marines, offering the Allies a vital airbase and important troop-staging area for the drive toward Japan. Adm. Halsey later stated, "Before Guadalcanal, the enemy advanced at his pleasure. After Guadalcanal, he retreated at ours." And with that, Guadalcanal took its place on history's pedestal. It's name would soon invoke a mythical reverence held by few battles in American history.

For Ron Spangler, of course, his fighting at Guadalcanal ended after being there for only a few months. Yet his struggle with malaria would continue for the next year. From Guadalcanal he was flown to a field hospital in New Haverti, where he stayed for a month. He then spent another three months receiving treatment in New Zealand. Finally, the chance came to rejoin his buddies in the field. "They came around and asked who wanted to go back to the States, and who wanted to go back to their outfit. I wanted to go back to my outfit. Then I came down with malaria again, because you would keep getting attacks of it, and they sent me back to San Diego."

San Diego would be his home for the next nine months. Three of those were spent in a hospital again as doctors tried to extinguish the recurring fevers and chills. To add salt to his healing wounds was the fact that he wasn't paid for eleven months due to a lack of pay records. He was given thirty days sick leave to travel back to Norfolk, but with no money he had to rely on an $85 loan from the Red Cross and a train ticket from his dad.

Still on the mend, he spent six months in a guard company at the San Diego Marine Base. "When I had that six months limited duty there, I had another malaria attack. Well, there was this doctor there doing some experimenting, and he shot some yellow looking stuff in my arm, and I never had another attack."

Back to fighting strength, he was transferred to the 4th Marine Division, which was soon to invade the islands of Saipan and Tinian. Saipan was only

*The last Japanese soldier to surrender at Guadalcanal did not do so until October 27, 1947, more than two years after Japan surrendered. He was one of many Japanese soldiers that lived in caves on various islands, unaware that the war had ended.

1,485 miles from Tokyo and capturing it would cut the enemy's supply and communication lines from Japan to her armed forces in the Southwest Pacific. It would also give the Americans a base from which to launch bombing runs against the main island of Japan. Guarding the vital base there were almost 30,000 Japanese soldiers that were dug into a highly developed system of defensive positions. Taking Saipan was going to be tough and bloody.

Once again, the Marines lived up to their creed of "First to Fight." Before they stormed ashore they were briefed on what they could expect. "In the surf," a medical officer commented, "beware of sharks, barracuda, sea snakes, anemones, razor-sharp coral, polluted waters, poison fish, and giant clams that shut on a man like a bear trap. Ashore, there is leprosy, typhus, filariasis, yaws, typhoid, dengue fever, dysentery, saber grass, insects, snakes, and giant lizards. Eat nothing growing on the island, don't drink its waters, and don't approach the inhabitants." Welcome to Saipan, boys.

On the morning of June 15, 1944, approximately 20,000 Marines hit the beaches at Saipan. Hitting back at them was a barrage of artillery and mortar fire, plus pockets of heavy machine-gun fire. Spangler states tersely that going in was "a pretty tough operation. We lost a lot of people." Spangler and his artillery crew made it onto the beaches unharmed, but there was nowhere to go once they got there. "We were pinned down that first night by the Japanese guns that were perched on a cliff. So the Navy shelled them all night long, so nothing could move all night, us or them. When those shells would come in, your pants would actually start flapping, they'd come so close. But the Navy knocked out a lot of those Japanese guns that night."

Spangler's artillery team was part of the force that was able to severely weaken the back of the Japanese defense over the next few weeks. His job was to either load the shell or pull the lanyard that sent the shell into the Japanese lines. "We'd fire some that would hit point blank, and others that would explode four to five feet above the ground. It was pretty hard to live through that. We figured one battalion of artillery in favorable ground could hold off 3,000 Japanese."

While the men up front took the worst punishment, there were some close calls in the gun pit in which Spangler was stationed. "They dropped a bomb and it knocked one of our big guns clean out of the pit. We had a guy named Joe Starper. He was at the gun right next to ours, and when I went to check on him he had been buried by all the dirt. But his feet were sticking out, so me and another guy had to hurry to dig him out before he suffocated.

"I never had to witness anyone being killed, but I saw an awful lot of dead being brought down past us. You don't visualize yourself laying there dead. You might say to yourself, 'That poor guy got it,' but if you thought about not making it you'd crack up. A lot of the guys that got too serious about it would have a nervous breakdown."

As the battle ground on, U.S. ground forces would be made to pay in blood for each hill and cave taken as they hacked their way through the island defenses. The Japanese had built mini-fortresses in the caves that honeycombed the island, and snipers hid in the fields of tall sugar cane. In Spangler's division, there was almost a 30-percent casualty rate. Some 5, 981 of Spangler's fellow 4th Division Marines were either killed, wounded, or listed as missing. As usual, Japanese losses were far greater, with over 23,000 known killed.

It was in the last few days of the Saipan battle that one of the war's most horrific acts took place. When the "American Devils," as the Japanese called us, reached the final neck of the island, thousands of Japanese civilians were flushed out of hiding. Some tried to surrender, yet were not allowed to by Japanese soldiers. Most simply refused to undergo the indignity and humiliation of surrender. Spangler describes with sorrow what he witnessed. "Our guys tried to get them to surrender, but the Japanese told them we would rape them and a whole bunch of other junk. We had loudspeakers set up trying to get them to give up, but they wouldn't. So whole families, even with their kids, would go up to these cliffs that faced the ocean. They'd cut the kids with a knife, then flip them out in the water. Then they'd do the same to themselves. Hundreds of them. It was the same way in the caves. You could hear the babies crying in there. We couldn't leave them behind our lines, so we had to close up the entrance with the demolition guys. Just buried them in there. It was either that or they'd take a flame thrower in there. And you know, a flame thrower doesn't have to hit you. It's so hot that it burns the oxygen out of the air and you suffocate."

Just two weeks later Spangler and the rest of the 4th Division would make another stab at the Japanese homeland by invading the island of Tinian, just south of Saipan. "We secured that place in a hurry," Spangler says. Even so, the stories from Tinian are similar to those from other islands: scores of Japanese committing banzai charges into Marine machine guns, with every hill and valley claiming more dead and wounded.

Next in line for Spangler and the 4th Division was Iwo Jima. And of all things, a life insurance policy kept Spangler out of harm's way. "I never did take out life insurance, because when I went in the pay was only $21 a month, and the life insurance was like $3.75. So I never took it out. Later, they pressed for it to people that didn't have it, but they wouldn't give it to me because of all the sick time I had had. So when we went into Iwo Jima, they put me into the rear echelon away from all the heavy fighting."

And that's where Spangler ended his war. While most of his buddies were decommissioned soon after being back in the States, he still had time left in his enlistment. He was dispatched to China to aid in the disarmament of the remaining Japanese. "We took all their weapons and then took all of their personal effects and put them in an envelope that we put around their neck. Then we sent them back to Japan. And the Japanese, once you ever capture one of them, they'll tell you everything you want to know, and they'll bow to you. Whatever you tell them to do, they'll double-time and do it.

"At this one compound that belonged to Esso Oil, the Japanese officers had riding horses. The ones we wanted we kept, and the ones we didn't we gave to the local farmers. So we had about seven or eight nice riding horses. And we had a Japanese veterinarian that we kept as long as we could, but they eventually sent him back, too. It was bad over there, though. You had to be careful. After the Japanese were gone, we guarded an ammunition depot. Of course, then we were guarding it from the communist Chinese that would raid the dump to steal ammo. We had one guy that got shot, but they weren't out to kill Americans. They just wanted the ammo. Anytime we went out on horses, we had to be in groups of six and you had to be armed because the people around there would rob you and steal your clothes. That was terrible duty there because you never got any rest. You'd be on eight hours, then off four. Then we still had to drill and patrol. And there wasn't any liberty because this little old town only had one place to go and eat. Everything else was out of bounds. And if you went into one of the villages, they'd all run in and lock their doors. They wouldn't associate with us even though we had liberated them.

"We couldn't even talk to a woman or we'd be court-martialed. That was because there was too much venereal disease. If you did get the V.D., when you got well they'd put you in the brig for thirty days for direct disobedience of an order. And that was the only place I was ever at in the Marine Corps where you could go in the PX and get a drink of whiskey. You could get drunk on a dollar. They didn't want us drinking Chinese whiskey because they made it out of all kinds of stuff.

"After that, they rotated us to a place called Tangu, which is where the battalion headquarters was. There, we served as guards on trains that had any kind of American possessions on them." After Tangu, Spangler's hitch was over and he was back in the States as a civilian. "The biggest mistake I made in my life was when I was getting discharged. They gave me a physical and the doctor said, "You have a loss of hearing. Why don't you stick around and get it evaluated. I said, 'No Sir! I want to go home!' So, I could've been drawing disability all this time."

After "fooling around" for a while, he considered reenlisting, but his father talked him out of it by getting him a job at the Norfolk Naval Operating Base as a laborer making thirty-five cents an hour. He ended up working there 37 years.

In 2001, as he reflects on the war and his feelings for the Japanese, he seems rather unemotional about the whole thing. "You talk to some guys, and they cry when they talk about it. It just never affected me that way. But I wasn't in the infantry, and they had the worst of it. I was lucky to be in the antitank and artillery." Maybe that's why his feelings toward the Japanese aren't as bitter as some. "I just don't have that feeling of hate. Back then, you just didn't think about them being human. It was like shooting a squirrel. You didn't have any feelings about it. I guess the Germans were the same way to the Americans in Europe."

"Semper Fidelis" is the motto for the United States Marine Corps. It means "Always Faithful." You see it on their flags, bumper stickers, recruitment ads, and T-shirts. On Ron Spangler, you see it in his face and hear it in his voice. As he said, "Patriotism, I guess."

1943

2001

He was chosen from thousands as one of the strongest and brightest. He was hardened by the toughest training our country could throw at him. From that training he went into enemy waters with little more than a knife. Today he would be called a Navy Seal. But as one of the first thirty of his kind, he was called a frogman.

Robert Kenworthy enlisted in the Navy in 1942 at the age of 19 because he was bored. His enlistment may have also been to fulfill a game he played as a child. "I remember when I was five or six, and I would be cutting the grass, I would pretend that each blade of grass was a German that I was mowing down. I had read and heard quite a few books about the Huns from World War I, so that's where that came from."

About the same time Kenworthy volunteered, a new, secret project was brewing in the cloak-and-dagger offices of the United States Military. What is now known as the CIA was in the early 1940s known as the OSS (Office of Strategic Services). Like today's CIA, it's purpose was to gather secret intelligence and to carry out sabotage missions. It was about to start a new way to do both.

The OSS had watched with great interest Italy's combat swimmers in the early months of World War II. Highly trained in reconnaissance and armed with small explosives, the Italian swimmers had been successful in raiding British ships. Not to be outdone, the OSS leadership was eager to get its own group of swimmers trained and into action. This elite group would be the United States' first-ever combat swimmers. They would be the mold that shaped today's U.S. Navy Seals, Army Ranger Scout Swimmers, U.S. Air Force Pararescuemen, and Combat Controllers. They would become America's first frogmen.

Recruitment was subtle. Small signs were posted in Army, Navy, Coast Guard, and Marine barracks across the country that simply read, "Wanted: Volunteers for Extra Hazardous Duty." The sign caught the attention of a young Robert Kenworthy. "People that volunteer for hazardous duty are a little bit different," he says with a knowing smirk. They would have to be different in at least the areas of IQ and strength. The OSS wanted only the top men from each branch. Of the 50,000 Navy men from which to choose, only two were selected. Robert Kenworthy was one. By mid-1943, thirty of America's finest, including Kenworthy, were sent to Camp Pendleton, California, for training that would not only change their lives, but the face of American special forces.

Training was brutal, unrelenting, and groundbreaking. The men were trained in waterborne infiltration, underwater demolitions, reconnaissance, small-boat work, navigation, small arms, hand-to-hand combat, judo, and silent killing. The finest equipment would be made available to them, including one of the world's first closed-circuit diving apparatuses, the Lambertsen Unit. It was developed to allow a well-trained combat swimmer to swim underwater bubble-free, permitting him to operate around target areas without a trace.

"The first day we had bayonet training, our instructor told us to take off the scabbards," Kenworthy says with a wry grin. "Now the biggest knife I had seen up to that point was a butter knife. He trained us to run full speed at the other guy, who would grab behind the bayonet, and hopefully put it past his ear, over his shoulder, then roll on his back, then stick his feet in the other fella. The first time you do that, it's very, very interesting."

Demolitions involved small, twelve-pound magnetic mines. Two of these small, yet effective, mines were attached to a swimmer, one on his front and one on his back. The men were taught how to attach these to a ship in order to sink it. "The thought of one man being able to destroy a destroyer or a cruiser seemed like a very notable thing. If you could take eight hundred men for one, that's a pretty good investment."

As their training progressed, so did the demands. Many exercises were performed at night, usually in the water. "We would be told to take a rubber boat, paddle it out about five miles (carrying a rifle and a sixty-six pound pack), come back into shore, then climb a mountain at dark, climb back down, paddle the boat out and back, and arrive back at 7 A.M. And in their extreme generosity, you had to clean your sidearm, then be cleaned up for a dress rehearsal of something at 8 A.M. It was the damndest thing. You don't realize how dark it really is until you're doing things like that."

All PT (physical training) was given under the presumption that a man could endure ten times the normal level of human endurance. Kenworthy and another man had been chosen to be the runners of the group, so they were told to run the last ten of their twenty mile marches.

And then there was the swimming. A lot of swimming. Since much of the men's time would be spent in the water during their upcoming missions, their swim training was gut-wrenching. They started each morning with a two-and-a-half-mile swim "just to warm up." And it wasn't in a pool. It was usually in the cold waters of the Pacific. "We had developed this ability to mesmerize ourselves as far as the coldness was concerned. But if you did it for more than two hours at a time, it was so cold that one or both of your testicles would climb back up inside. And it's OK when they go up, but when they come down, oh! I've seen some of these fellows all bent over just screaming. Oh, those were the good old days!"

All of these assaults on the human mind and spirit were meant to weed out the weaker men. "Every few days someone would fall out. The competition was terrific between the men." The thought of quitting was never an option for Kenworthy, but an accident with a swim board one afternoon almost took that decision out of his hands.

The accident occurred during a training exercise using swimboards, big nine-foot boards that resemble surfboards. One of his crew members' boards came shooting out of the surf and slammed into Kenworthy's face, striking him just below the nose. He was knocked unconscious and left floating limp in the surf. A team member pulled him ashore. He recovered quickly, but was told that he would lose his four front teeth. He's proud of the fact that he kept those teeth, but did have to have them capped.

Keeping a regular sleep schedule was a different story. "When you're up all night and up all day, you don't think about time," says Kenworthy. "But every two weeks we would be granted a long weekend, Thursday through Sunday. Those were times to kick up your heels." That meant traveling to nearby Hollywood where they often were afforded special treatment due to their affiliation with the OSS. Hedda Hopper, the famous gossip columnist of the time, usually arranged hotel rooms for them. They were also treated to restaurant service by stars such as Bette Davis at the Hollywood Guild Canteen.

Of course, in the midst of most straining, stressful situations are the light-hearted stories which stand the test of time. Kenworthy's involves a goat. "One day, Jerry Bevaty and I decided to climb a mountain of a few thousand feet. Jerry was an interesting person. If he had to go anywhere, he would put anything he was carrying in his mouth and walk on his hands. He was solid muscle. Anyhow, when we got to the top we found a mountain goat path a few inches wide and there was a family of goats there. We wanted to catch one.

"It appeared that the path went around the crown of the mountain so we decided that Jerry, being the more surefooted, would follow them around the mountain and drive them back around into my waiting hands. I found a place just below the path with two gnarled, stunted pines about two feet apart and barely enough room on the rocks below for each foot. There was a three hundred to four hundred drop below. I waited there for twenty minutes clutching a pine tree with each hand.

"Then I heard rumbling and shouting and then saw Jerry flailing his arms trying to keep his balance on that thin trail as he chased the goats to me. I let the papa pass, then the mama. As the third kid passed I grabbed it with my right hand. When I did that, my feet slipped off the rock and there I was with a good grip on a tree with my right hand, a writhing, squirming dynamite of a goat in my left, and nothing below me. I shouted to Jerry, who helped me subdue the little goat. We finally got it down to the camp and it became the mascot and a wonderful pet to us all." That's how the OSS swimmers blew off a little steam.

By late 1943 their training at Camp Pendleton and Catalina Island was moved to a secluded island in the Bahamas. There they were taught advanced training in clandestine underwater operations. They shared the island with British soldiers, who also had facilities there. "That was the most wonderful place I had been and oddly enough I felt at home there, like I belonged there. I had never felt at home where I was born and raised.

"There, we had fabulous, wonderful, wonderful training. We slept on the beach at night and when the first one inch of light would appear on the horizon, you would struggle out of your mummy bag and you'd run down this dock, dive in the water, and wake up when you were ten feet down. That is the most wonderful way in the world to wake up!

"But one day something a bit hair-raising happened during one of our skin dives. I was in about twelve feet of water and looking down before diving again when suddenly a school of small fish started rushing by and I noticed they were being passed by bigger fish. So I wondered why the rush and turned around to see this five foot or so barracuda slam on his brakes only five to six feet from me. Just a few days before, a native fisherman had died within twenty-four hours after being bitten by one of those scavengers that are near-sighted but lightning fast. So for the seventy-five yards to shore, I back paddled very slowly while that barracuda followed me as his mouth slowly opened and closed, opened and closed."

Barracuda's aside, Kenworthy takes us through a typical training operation the men performed while at the Bahamas: "I remember I could see this sentry up above this dock and I had to come in from the water without a ripple or a bubble. It probably took me close to two hours to get off my fins, my Lambertsen Unit off, and then to go all the way around the sentry. Turned out here was this British colonel and I came up behind him, put my knife between his shoulders and said, 'You're dead.' He was very impressed that we could do that." During this time Kenworthy also taught himself how to swim with only one arm in case he was hit on one side. "That way I wouldn't swim around in circles."

When asked if his teammates were eager to put their training into action, he answers by telling a story about their trainer, a Capt. Sullivan. Sullivan had already seen combat, and seemed to have been affected deeply by it. Each night, alone, Sullivan would spend time in a rocking chair with a bottle of scotch and two packs of Camel cigarettes. Kenworthy says his team could see what combat had done to him, but they were still eager. "You don't volunteer for especially hazardous duty unless you want some excitement." They would not have to wait much longer.

By June 1944 the Allies were making their big push against Hitler's Atlantic Wall, yet Kenworthy's swimmer group (initially, there were five) was sent to the Pacific. Their first stop was in Hawaii, where something took place that Kenworthy still smolders over. In an effort to consolidate forces, the elite OSS swimmers were merged with the Navy's Underwater Demolition Teams (UDT), now known worldwide as the UDT-Seals. Despite the present-day mystique and respect the UDT-Seals now evoke, Kenworthy said at the time he was "disgusted" by the merger. "We had been chosen over a lot of men, and we were exceptional. And we felt in almost every way of looking at it that we were superior."

Regardless, their mission remained the same. For their first operation, several members of Kenworthy's Swimmer Group I, not including Kenworthy, were dropped off by submarine for a reconnaissance mission on the Island of Yap, southeast of the Philippines. Kenworthy recalls that the swimmers completed their reconnaissance and started to make their way back to the submarine. Three of the men did not arrive at the rendezvous point on time.

According to Kenworthy, the swimmers who had returned to the submarine thought they could see the other rubber boat coming from a few hundred yards away in the darkness. They asked the submarine's captain to wait, he refused, and the other three men were left behind. The men were rumored to have been captured by the Japanese, tortured to death by the traditional "death of a thousand cuts," then decapitated. According to the Navy Seals, "the actual fate of these men is still subject to speculation. It is not at all clear that these men were 'executed' by the Japanese. In fact, one story has it that they were captured and taken on board a Japanese ship, which was later sunk by the U.S. Navy." Regardless of how the men died, the Seals recently decided to name a pool after them...fifty-five years after their deaths.

However killed, one of the men was a friend of Kenworthy's. "Bob Black and I played golf together at the Lincoln Golf Course in San Francisco the day before we shipped out. After we finished playing I remember we were having a drink, looking out across the Pacific at the setting sun, and I said to him, prophetically to say the least, 'I wonder if we'll ever play golf here again?' Three months later he was gone. That fellow was such a nice guy, and had such a horrible end. It was revolting to me." I asked him if he still holds a grudge for the Japanese because of that. He tersely stated, "I had a Jap skull for an ash tray after they cut off the head of my buddy."

I also asked Kenworthy if the fate of his friend haunted him during his later missions. He shook his head and said, "If you start thinking about things like that, you're going to fox yourself out." But he did mention that Tokyo Rose, the sweet-voiced Japanese woman who played American music and spouted Japanese war propaganda to the Allied troops, was a bit unnerving. "Tokyo Rose would come on the Mosquito Network in Guadalcanal and she'd say, 'We know where you frogmen are going to land. We'll have two Japanese swimmers waiting for each one of you.' They never did, but it was very disconcerting."

As the Allied forces fought northward towards Japan in their island-hopping campaign in 1944, the Palau Islands, a small string of islands southeast of the Philippines, were marked for invasion by the Allies. At the bottom of the string was a dot of an island named Anguar, which happens to mean "bird dropping." It was the island on which the Japanese mined most of their phosphorous for artillery shells and fertilizer. It was also the place that Kenworthy had the most "interesting and memorable" day of his life.

Kenworthy and his partner were sent into the waters off Anguar four days before the invasion. Their mission was to mark the water depths and any obstacles along the approach route to the beach that the landing craft would use. They would also search for mines to be destroyed closer to D-Day (invasion day). Swimmers were paired and given five hundred yards of beach to cover per pair. They were given no protection, no cover.

To get close to the beach was quite a feat. "For the drop-offs, we would get along the gunnels of these little boats, LCPs (landing craft personnel), and at the right moment we would be tapped on the shoulder and we would go right up in the air as far as we could. Then we would duck our heads with our face plates on so we wouldn't splatter glass all over our faces, and then we'd roll into the water. This was while we were going 40 mph. That way, the Japs didn't have long enough to shoot you."

The drop-offs would take place several hundred yards out from the beach. Once in the water, the pair would swim towards the beach to begin work. One man would do the diving while the other would stay at the surface with a plexiglass grid to mark any notations that were needed. Because good visibility was a must, all of this was done in daylight, right in front of the Japanese gun emplacements. Kenworthy's swimmer group made eight separate trips into the beach before the invasion began, all without being noticed by the enemy.

D-Day at Anguar was September 17, 1944. While many of his memories of that day aren't pleasant, a few come to mind that seem rather unique. One of Kenworthy's most vivid memories is of eating breakfast before the mission and watching the operating tables being set up. "It's really something to visualize yourself on an operating table as you're trying to eat. I can't convey what that does to one." His other, seemingly tangential anecdote involved cockatoos. "I guess there were thousands of cockatoos that were dislodged from their homes, those beautiful birds. I could see them flying all over the island. I didn't think much about the Japanese, but I did think a lot about those cockatoos."

Early that morning, Kenworthy and his partner were put into the water to blast holes through the coral reef to allow clear passage for the landing craft. It's at this point that Kenworthy says, "All hell broke loose." As Kenworthy looked toward the beach, he saw three Japanese soldiers. They had seen him, too. He then saw them pull away the fronds of a palm tree, revealing a machine gun pillbox. The pillbox opened fire. Then there was more fire from the right side of the beach. There was nowhere to go and nowhere to hide. They tried to conceal themselves in the bullet-riddled water as best they could by only surfacing long enough to catch a quick gulp of air. "A very strange thing happens when you're under fire. You'd be surprised how long it can seem in a very short period. The faster things move, the more slowly they seem to move." Fortunately for the men, either a heavy cruiser or a nearby gun boat destroyed the gun emplacements.

But it wasn't over yet. They were then mistakenly strafed by cannon fire by one of their own planes. As Kenworthy takes a moment to either calm the anger or hold back the fear he felt at that time, he quietly says, "We made lewd signs at them as they pulled away." Despite the attacks on them from both sides, Kenworthy and the rest of the swimmers were able to make it back to the ship, their jobs completed. At least they thought so.

Following the marked paths created by the swimmers, the Army landed. The early going was tough. Japanese resistance was stiff and the Americans had only moved two hundred yards in from the beach by afternoon. Wanting to bolster their forces on the beach, the Navy ordered the swimmers back to Anguar, except this time not in the water, but onto the beach in a foxhole. "We'd already been in there twice on D-Day minus four, twice on D-Day minus three, twice on D-Day minus two, twice on D-Day minus one. We had been driven out of the water once by sharks, and were right there on D-Day. So, on D-Day afternoon they took several of us, gave us bayonets, and stuck us on the beach to protect it. And here were all these sailors and Army men still out there on their ships. Hadn't we done enough of our part, yet?! Can you understand how we felt?!"

The fighting continued through the night. "The next morning, in the cold, gray light of dawn, when I looked at the beach I could just see two Americans huddled behind burned out halftracks." Despite the slow start at Anguar, the island was captured in less than a week. Some 260 Americans were killed there, more than 1,350 were wounded. The swimmers escaped unharmed.

"When I think about the war, it's usually of Anguar. I became a man there, or aged a great deal, or saw things differently afterwards. Probably all three."

A few weeks later the frogmen were called upon again at the island of Ulithi. Just north of Anguar, Ulithi was part of eight islands on the crest of a volcano. "As we swam in, I was overjoyed. I could pick out the men's huts and various other things, and it was just fabulous. After seeing that I decided I wanted to quit the service right then and have many books mailed to me there. I could have spent a few years there, relaxing and reading."

In terms of combat, Ulithi was the opposite of Anguar. The Japanese had evacuated during the invasion of the Palau islands, so there was no resistance, except for something that remains a bit of a mystery. "As we did our reconnaissance, we got closer and closer. My buddy was down below taking the readings, and I was there making a notation, and all of a sudden, SWOOSH! right by my ear. When he came up, I said 'Dell, something strange just happened. Something just went by my ear. I didn't hear a report from a rifle.' And while we were talking, another SWOOSH!" They never figured out exactly what it was that was fired at them, but speculate that it was from a native's bow and arrow.

One of the few casualties Kenworthy was aware of at Ulithi was the island chief's daughter. "She picked up some shrapnel in her chest and was brought on board with her father. She had tattoos of sharks in three little rows that were neatly done in some sort of vegetable dye. We learned that children on the island at the age of thirteen were allowed to sit on the outskirts of the council and then get their first row on their wrists. As they grew, more were added. Unfortunately, the chief's daughter died."

Her death seems to symbolize Kenworthy's lament over the destruction that war, and the Americans, had done to the picturesque island. "A year later we were back at Ulithi and I was disgusted. Those people had been so happy before. We were the first Caucasians there in over a quarter-century." The sight of the American fleet there, the beer cans that littered the beach, the intrusive housing, all had marred an island that had offered no real resistance.

By November 1944 the U.S. was on it's way to the Philippines to fulfill MacArthur's promise of "I shall return." Kenworthy was tapped to be a part of that return. But on his way there a typhoon hit, sinking four ships. Kenworthy, who had spent the better part of the last two years in the water, says he was so seasick he could hardly eat anything for four days.

As the fleet arrived in the Philippine's Leyte Gulf, the storm moved from the sea to the sky. "One night, just as the sun was going down blood-red, here came five kamikazes right out of that blood-red sun. As they got closer, one was coming right at us and I could see the Jap's goggles while he was strafing us. Next to me and my friend was this great big cook who was manning a .50 caliber machine gun. He froze. My friend jumped over the edge and cold-cocked this cook in the neck and took over the machine gun." Kenworthy doesn't remember what happened afterwards, mainly due to the blur in numbers of kamikaze attacks they had in the upcoming weeks. At times, they numbered one hundred per day.

One scare, though, is hard to forget. "One of the suicide planes managed to break through the antiaircraft fire and scrape the ship. I felt this jolt and instantly knew what had happened." The Zero had grazed the ship's fantail with a wing, yet only minor damage was done.

Mission number three, which was supposed to be Kenworthy's last, was to reconnoiter one of the islands in Leyte Gulf. "As we approached the beach, the coxswain of our LCP passed within forty yards of the first fish trap we had ever seen. It was a circle of countless bamboo poles. It was almost our undoing as a Japanese mortar shell dropped in the middle of the trap followed repeatedly by others. After many near misses, they decided to conserve their ammo for the invasion.

"As we swam into the beach, the water was murky and it took us forever to check for mines. We could only see about five feet and had to stand on our heads as only the bottom two feet gave us any decent visibility. We found no mines.

"We ended up going in several times on that operation, but it was one time in particular that could have been a turning point in my life. My partner King and myself were about seven hundred yards from the beach when we were instructed to swim in and reconnoiter what was believed to be an ammunition dump. Meanwhile, I had been watching salvos from the heavy cruiser *Denver*. I counted seven of them that were long. I figured she would probably then shoot short, then center in between the long and the short. It was the short I was worried over. I debated this in not so diplomatic terms, but we were sent in anyhow.

"King and I had started to swim in when a whole broadside from the *Denver* hit just ahead of us. Thanks to the delay from our little debate we were just far enough away so that our intestines were saved from the worst part of the impact. The speed of sound in water is 4,850 ft/sec, and the force is fantastic. I told King we must never let that happen again."

Kenworthy's team was then sent to Guam and placed on standby for the invasion of Iwo Jima. Their station on Guam sat below mountains that still hid hundreds of Japanese soldiers. Although hidden, the Japanese made a point to let the small American camp know they were there.

"From time to time we would hear a strange drama. We would see a cross burn up in those hills, and when the wind was right we could hear their chanting. During the session they would chose one or more of their soldiers to come down to our camps to try to slit our throats. There were fifteen Americans that suffered that fate while I was there.

"It kept us a little nervous, and after intervals of this there would be a wind which came up a ravine which brought out their voices saying, 'Here they come.' It was especially audible on those dark, dark nights on guard duty.

"One day we tired of those hecklers in the hills and decided to go up after them, some fifteen of us. I guess some of my former correct decisions were recognized so our only Tompson machine gun was shoved into my hands to lead the group. I decided it would be foolish to go straight up and would be better to circumvent the hill. The grass was dry and a few inches over our heads. Picking my way slowly and quietly through, suddenly two deer jumped in front of us. There were harsh whispers behind me telling me to shoot them, but I held up my hand for quiet. I thought that firing into that dry grass would set off a fire, clearly showing our position. At that moment, shots rang out from up above us, and we decided it would be best to head back."

Back to the United States is where Kenworthy thought he was heading. At least that's what he was told. Prior to their first mission, the swimmers had been told that if they survived three missions, they would be sent back home. Evidently, the need for swimmers was such that the promise was conveniently forgotten. But not by the swimmers. It's a subject that still brings out a grudge streak, fiercely angering Kenworthy. "If you ever see the picture Richard Widmark made about us frogmen, you will see something about a mutiny. That was us in Team 10. We were disgusted that we were taken out of the OSS and put into the UDT with nothing said to us. Also, after our three missions, they told us we had to do two more. So, we mutinied. I finally got sent back, but not until I did two more missions."

The first of those two was on the big island in the Lingayen Gulf. "The beach we reconnoitered showed nothing. Not a tree, house, bush, man or animal, so not a shot was heard.

"After our operation, Bodine and I followed up the Army on D-Day by 200-300 yards and came to a gravel road. As we approached the road a jeep was coming towards us from the left and a Jap Zero was also coming down the road. We jumped in a ditch and watched the Jap strafe the road around the jeep. In that jeep was MacArthur and his driver. Neither one of them batted an eye. As Kipling said, 'You are a better man than I am, Gunga Din.'"

After his final mission at Subic Bay, which he says was a "snap," Kenworthy was finally on his way home. The first few months were restless ones. He had difficulty sleeping and usually spent part of the night just sitting in the barrack's bathroom. He was put on report several times for this. Finally, another officer heard about the behavior and asked for Kenworthy's military record. After reading it, he told the officer who was writing the reports, "If you had been where he was you probably couldn't sleep either. Get off his back and he'll be fine."

The sleepless nights went away, but Kenworthy had had enough of the Navy. He says he couldn't have stayed in the Navy anyhow. "If you want to take a beachhead, I'm your guy. But I'm not one for shuffling papers."

And he wasn't one for settling down in the States, either. For fifteen years he traveled and worked in Africa and Italy. Despite those travels, the U.S. government tracked him down in 1960. "We had barely settled in Rome when I got a letter on that funny brown paper from the Selective Service. They asked a lot of questions like 'Do you speak Spanish? What is the condition of your health?' I didn't like it at all. I had never joined a reserve.

"When I mailed it back in, I forgot to put a stamp on it with no return address on it. Well, in 1961 another letter arrived from them saying that due to an oversight on my part my reply was greatly delayed and asked me some questions I can't recall. Come to find out, they wanted me for the Bay of Pigs invasion. The whole thing was a fiasco due to improper, if any, reconnoitering. The bottoms of the three of the invading boats were ripped out. I felt a little guilty, but as the Italians say, "The smell of the fish starts at the head!"

Then, a few years later, he was approached by the South African government to help train their military against invasion. "My background was perfect since I had been working all over Africa (selling large pipes). I knew the waters and countries, the ins and outs, but I had other things planned for life."

Those other things have taken Kenworthy on a road leading far away from the military mindset. Reveling in the spiritual world now, he has trained as a shaman healer, has searched, and found, his "guide," and claims to have lived many lives before, mostly as Native Americans.

Despite what he sees as his continuing thread through the ages, his blip in time during the war still lingers vividly. "The horrible thing about the training we received is that in the few times I've had a bit of difficulty since World War II, when you know how to dance and the music starts, it's virtually instantaneous. You're a walking time bomb." Meaning, in the few times that he's been threatened physically, the other man has paid dearly.

But now, in his late 70s, his biggest threat seems to be the removal of skin cancers caused by too many hours in the sun during his training and missions. A fellow teammate recently had to have his ears removed. Yet, through voracious reading and nightly meditation, his memories still remain clear. He does admit, "As time goes on you tend to forget the bad parts, and relish other parts that have depth and flavor. I just don't think or talk about the war even when we swimmers are together. It was a shock to me to look in the eyes of the twenty or so dead Japanese I saw during the war that had been trying to kill us. Out of our small group we had several men that cracked up and just could not go on anymore. For me, though, I'm happy that we had the utmost of thrills without having to do the killing."

Robert Kenworthy has a library of stories that could only be compiled from a lifetime of experiences that few among us are either blessed, or cursed, with. In fact, those stories could take up quite a few more pages in this book. Part of that log of personal history is his eventual move to Virginia Beach, home of the Atlantic Fleet's UDT-Seals. His move to Hampton Roads had nothing to do with that, though. He moved here simply to be with a woman he loved.

For years, the OSS and its frogmen seemed largely forgotten in the reams of history's chronicles of World War II. But more than fifty years later, in the late 1990s, their legacy and foundation in the annals of U.S. Special Forces were commemorated with a memorial stone at the Army Special Operations Forces Plaza at Fort Bragg, North Carolina. Kenworthy made the trip to Fort Bragg, donned his green beret, and walked among his fellow legends. Legends they truly are.

1944                                            2000

The first time I saw Maggie Lowrance was on television. She was dressed in an American Legion Uniform that was soaked with rain. The wind blew hard against the other women and men who stood beside her at the Tidewater Veteran's Memorial on Memorial Day, 2000. Despite the weather, she and a handful of others were determined to pay homage to those who had given their lives for our country. She stood there not only as a proud American, but also as a woman who had been one of the pioneers in naval history.

Before World War II women had basically been shut out of men's wars. The few women who fought in the American Revolution and America's Civil War often did so dressed as men. By World War I women were brought in as Navy nurses and yeomanettes, and as support for Marines. By the beginning of World War II women's groups, led in part by the President's wife, Eleanor Roosevelt, demanded that women be given a stronger, more permanent role in their country's military service.

Hesitantly, Congress and America gave in and women flocked to the recruiting stations. Auxiliary units for each branch of the service were created, allowing women to serve as technicians, secretaries, supply clerks, mechanics, and in a variety of other roles that needed filling due to the dwindling numbers of available men. What followed was a litany of acronyms. The first such group during the war was the WAACS (Women's Army Auxiliary

Corps), later termed the WACS (Women Army Corps). The WACS were nearly 100,000 strong by the end of the war. Women also enlisted in the WAAFS (Women's Auxiliary Air Forces), WAFS (Women's Auxiliary Ferrying Squadron), WASPS (Women's Air Force Service Pilots), SPARS (women members of the U.S. Coast Guard, their name derived from the Guard's motto Semper Paratus, "always ready"), and the auxiliary units for the Marines, nicknamed by some as BAMs, or "broad-assed marines."

For the Navy, July 30, 1942 was the turning point for women. That's when President Roosevelt changed the course of naval history by signing the Navy Women's Reserve Act. From this law swelled the WAVES, Women Accepted for Volunteer Emergency Service. When the war ended, there were 84,000 WAVES serving across the country as mechanics, pilots, office assistants, hospital corpsmen, radio operators, and cooks. They were the Navy's home-front soldiers. One of those was Maggie Lowrance.

Born in Chicago and raised in Mountain Lakes, New Jersey, Margaret Lowrance was destined to do something different from the other girls on her street. "I was mechanically inclined. I could take something apart and put it back together, and my brother couldn't. My dad always said I could have been an engineer," Lowrance boasts.

But in her late teens she found herself doing the work that most other young women in the early 1940s were given: clerical work. She commuted to downtown New York City for more than two years to work in the secretary department at Western Electric. Then came Pearl Harbor and with it changes in the American work force and military that would last through today.

"It was a Sunday night when we heard about the attack. I was sitting out on the front step with my mother when Daddy heard it on the radio. I went to work the next day at the AT&T building in downtown New York. They got us all in the big lobby when Roosevelt made his famous speech. Somehow they piped it through the whole building. The next day all the recruiters were filled with people enlisting. The whole world seemed to be going crazy. It was kind of an unreal time.

"We had blackout curtains since we weren't that far from the coast. We had drill sirens, and my father was a block captain who patrolled the neighborhood to make sure the curtains were drawn and the lights were out. My mother was in the WAACS, driving admirals and generals back and forth into New York City two days a week. And I remember Bundles for Britain that people would put together since they were being bombed. We saved scrap metal, newspapers, and bottles. It was like how we do recycling now. The war was always on everybody's mind. There were flags all over the place. We were a flag-waving nation in those days.

"After I joined the service and I would go home on leave, I would go down to an office in Hackensack and get my food-ration stamps that I was to use while I was home. Well, I would give those to my mother so she could have extra gas, extra meat, extra everything. Also, we didn't drive our cars much during the war. We did an awful lot of walking or we took the bus."

Caught in the fervor of patriotism shooting across America, Lowrance wanted to do her part. But one thing held her back initially: her father. "At the time, my father was trying to get back into the service. He had been in the reserves after World War I as a captain. But when he tried to get back in, they found something wrong with his eyes, which turned out to be glaucoma."

Daughter Maggie kept her desires to join a secret until her father was denied service. "I would not have gone in if he had been accepted because I had a mother and a baby sister and my grandmother. I would not have left them alone with my dad being gone. Plus, my brother had already joined the Army. So I didn't say anything until he told us he couldn't get in. I then said, 'I want to go in the Navy!' Daddy said, 'Oh, that is a lark!' He was all for it even though he was an Army man. As for my mother, she very reluctantly signed the papers. She didn't want me to go."

Even with the country's fervent nationalistic pride, there were few women with the same intentions as Lowrance. She didn't know of anyone in her high school graduating class, or at Western Electric, who had joined the newly formed women's units. Their reluctance may not have been completely their own.

"A lot of men who had girlfriends who wanted to join the WAVES did not approve. In fact, I was engaged at the time to a fella who was in the Army Air Corps. When I told him I was going to enlist in the WAVES, he said, 'Well, I don't think you will, but when I get home we'll talk about it.' So I said to myself, 'I'm not too sure I want to be engaged to someone who's telling me what to do with my life before I marry him because that means he'll always tell me what to do and I'm not going to put up with that.' I waited until he got home, but I did break off the engagement."

Still aware of the pervasive skepticism of women being in the military, Maggie Lowrance enlisted in the Navy in March of 1943. "I wanted to get in there. I knew what they wanted us for, and I wanted to see what I could do to help. Plus, my brother was in the service. My mother already had one star in the window and I wanted to give her another.

"When I joined, we were not allowed outside the continental U.S., but I had to promise my father if it became otherwise, I would not go. I would have faithfully kept that promise." It was a promise easy to keep. Not until early 1945 were WAVES personnel allowed to leave the States, and then they were restricted to Alaska and Hawaii.

After her induction into the United States Navy, Lowrance was sent on one of the "petticoat trains" to Hunter College in New York for three weeks of boot camp. Hunter College had been completely taken over by the Navy for the sole purpose of training women. Compared to what many of the women were used to, even during the depression, living conditions were crowded and generally unpleasant. It was no powder-puff camp.

"Our boot camp was just like the men's, except it wasn't as physically tortuous. We did have drills every day, though. We learned how to fire a rifle. We were told that when you aim a gun, you either shoot to kill, or you don't shoot. Our drill instructors were male Marines. They generally treated us nice, but they weren't soft on us. We also had studies every day about the seagoing service. We had to take math, learn the different ships of the line and the different aircraft, and we were tested on all of that.

"Then we were given overall aptitude tests, and from that they put us where they thought we belonged. Luckily I got what I wanted, and that was mech (mechanics) school. I would have been disappointed if I had been assigned to a clerical position, because I had done that for two-and-a-half years in one form or another." After they were assigned to their various schools, the female sailors were dispatched across the country for more training. Lowrance was sent to Oklahoma.

"This was wartime, and you couldn't divulge where you were being sent. So I couldn't tell my mother where I was going. But I had a way of letting her know. She knew I wanted to go to mech school, and there were two of them. One was in Memphis, and the other was in Norman, Oklahoma. My brother was stationed in Oklahoma, so when I called to tell her where I was going, I said, 'I'm going to go see Tom.' So she knew where I was going to be stationed without me telling her."

Lowrance left Hunter College as a second class seaman, and boarded a general troop train that ran to Canada to Detroit to Chicago and then finally to Norman. There were men on the train, but they were kept away from the women. Lowrance comments there was "no coed anything" back then.

Lowrance spent the next six months at the Naval Air Technical Training Center in Norman being trained as an aviation machinist's mate. For a woman, it was work that was unheard of at that time. Lowrance points out, "You may have found a woman doing that kind of work in a private garage, but that was usually only if they had graduated from high school without office skills.

"At mech school, we learned everything about the planes and the engines. It was much more detailed than what we learned in boot camp. To work on the planes and engines, we learned how to safety wire things, how to put cylinders on, how to measure torque on our torque wrench, how to time an engine, and a few other things. Most of the men that were our instructors really enjoyed teaching the women because most of us were really intent on doing things well.

"While we were there, some of the Marines that had been at Guadalcanal were stationed there. We got to know a lot of them. Some of them wanted to talk and some of them didn't. But we were there to listen if they did. I had also heard that I had lost a couple of my classmates from high school. All of us were 17 and 18 when we graduated in 1940, and probably ninety percent of the boys went into the service."

Lowrance says she loved her time in Norman and has since been back to visit the Training Center. "Almost 50 years after we had been there we could still look around and tell which building was which. We had a wonderful time there."

By mid-1944, it was time for Lowrance to put her skills to work. She was assigned to Corpus Christi, Texas, for A&R, Assembly and Repair. "I had been on leave in New Jersey and then met my friends in Chicago. I celebrated my 21st birthday on the train ride down to Houston. From Chicago to Houston we had a train car full of nothing but men and women service people. We had a ball. We had a birthday party for twelve hours!"

Once in Corpus Christi it was time for Lowrance to join the ranks of Rosie the Riveter. Rosie the Riveter was the female icon of the day, an attractive yet determined woman dressed in a denim work shirt with the sleeves rolled up, hair wrapped in a red bandana, and wrench in hand. She was used as a selling tool to get women into the factories to replace the men. But she also served as an appropriate symbol for the change in how America viewed its women, at least in the workplace. The difference between Rosie and Maggie was that at the end of the day Rosie supposedly went home to a house. Maggie went back to her barracks.

With thousands of other WAVES, Maggie donned her cap and overalls and went to work. "What we did was get on an assembly line. After each broken engine had been taken apart and reworked, they were given to us. We started at the very bottom and rebuilt them along the assembly line. They moved me from one position to another until it got to the point that I knew how to put the whole engine together. I really enjoyed the work, I did it well, and I learned it quickly."

Being moved around worried Lowrance for many months. "I felt like, 'Am I not doing well here? Is that why they're sending me somewhere else?' I just had the feeling I wasn't doing as well as they wanted me to. But I mentioned that to my husband after I got out of the service and he told me that meant they were grooming me to eventually make chief. That made me feel really good." To this day she can still rattle off the engine sizes and into which planes they went.

It was in Corpus Christi that she met Jim Lowrance, a fellow serviceman. They met shortly after her arrival there, but after three to four months together, he was transferred to Norfolk. Having fallen in love, the two kept in touch through letters. Jim came back to Corpus Christi to visit Maggie. The day after he arrived they were standing in front of the base chaplain getting married. The next time she would see him would be six months later.

"At that time, you could stay in if you were married. But before then, if they found out you were married, you had to get out. I had a girlfriend that did that. But if you were pregnant, then you had to get out."

The Lowrances met in New Jersey for their leave in September, 1944. Within a few months, she knew she was pregnant. "I wasn't expecting it, but we only had weekends together. I was happy about the baby and being able to go home, but I knew my mom and dad would be a little bit disappointed that I wasn't able to stay in the Navy until the war was over."

Lowrance hid her pregnancy from the Navy until January of 1945. Five months pregnant, she revealed her secret by going to the WAVES clinic for a pregnancy test. Her pregnancy confirmed, she was ordered to stay in the clinic until her papers for dismissal were cleared. She received a discharge from the United States Navy "...for the good of the service under honorable conditions."

In October of 1945 Maggie moved to Norfolk, where Jim was stationed. She's been there since. Although she was in the service for less than two years, Jim stayed for 24. She feels as though the Navy has been her life, not only because of her husband's career, but also because of what she's done since the WAVES.

"In the late 50s, I guess there must have been eight to ten of us who were military wives. Our husbands were still in the service here and we all knew each other. Well, we decided to just start getting together, and we went out to this place at Little Creek that the Navy base let us have. We met, and we decided to do it again. So in a couple of months we called each other. Then we got a couple of more women to join us. So we just kept meeting every three months on the last Sunday of the month and had lunch.

"We kept staying together, and gradually people heard about us until we got to be quite a big organization. In the 60s we were incorporated with the state of Virginia as a non-profit organization, and we had a charter and a set of bylaws."

The name of the organization is the Tidewater Silver Salts. It continues to be a dedicated group of former, active, and retired Navy, Coast Guard, and Marine women. Lowrance says they're more of a social organization than anything else, yet they have started a scholarship for female high school seniors that have or had a mother or grandmother in the Navy.

The Silver Salts, with Lowrance as President, boarded a bus and headed to Washington, D.C., in October of 1997. It was a day many had awaited for a long time. They were there to honor the dedication of the Women in Military Service for America Memorial. Standing at the gateway to Arlington National Cemetery, where Lowrance's husband is buried, the Memorial is the first to honor the nearly two million women who have served in all branches of the U.S. Armed Forces since the American Revolution.

Also at the Memorial were service women who owe a debt of gratitude to women like Maggie Lowrance. Today's women in the military have opportunities, and respect, that the WAVES were never given. Imagine what the women in the WAVES would have thought had they been told that one day a woman would be captain of a Navy cruiser. Or that women would fly jets off carrier decks. A look of skepticism would surely have come over their faces. But in realizing how far they had come by 1945, they may have sensed that it was inevitable, and needed.

I asked Lowrance how she feels about women in combat, or in submarines. "I'm still torn about that. I just don't know. I don't mind them being on ships of the line. I'm rather proud of that. And I don't mind them flying, but I don't want to see them in submarines."

In 2001, Maggie Lowrance is as patriotic as she was when she went down to the recruiting office in 1943. Two American flags adorn her home in Norfolk. "I'm a flag waiver. I'm a pretty patriotic person and I really love it." Does she see that patriotism in today's America? Yes and no. "When we were out there on Memorial Day there were less than 200 people. There should have been a lot more. Yes, we were in miserable weather that day. But what I was thinking about was that was nothing compared to what the soldiers, in any war, had to go through.

"But I still think the current generation of American youth would rise if they were called to duty. In my everyday life I don't see what the news shows us in terms of the bad things that some people do. I think at least 80-90 percent are good."

Maggie Lowrance certainly stepped forward when America called. Along with hundreds of thousands of other women across the country, she made the commitment to serve, and if necessary protect, a country that still wasn't comfortable with that role. For that pioneering spirit and her willingness to serve when needed, we are grateful.

# D-DAY

## PART I

## WILLIAM WILLIAMSON

1944

2000

Some have called it the most important day of the twentieth century. In the least, it was perhaps the most important day of World War II. It was the day in which freedom's "fury of a democracy," as Eisenhower called it, would bear it's full might and hurl itself against fascism's Atlantic Wall. On that one day, a generation's mettle would be tested by death, hardened by heroism, destined through determination. The world knows that day simply as D-Day, but William "Buck" Williamson knows it as the day "it all went wrong."

The walls of Buck Williamson's den are dotted with framed certificates, pictures, maps, and medals, many of which reveal what he went through on June 6, 1944. When I met him, he was wearing a shirt that read, "Some Gave All." Many of those around him on D-Day did. Before he began to tell me his story, he gave me a small plastic globe that contained merely a handful of sand from Omaha Beach. It now sits on my desk at home, and whenever it catches it my eye, I think not only of Buck Williamson, but of the nearly 175,000 men who, in one morning, turned the tide of the war.

His service to our country started more out of selfish, rather than selfless, need. As a junior at Maury High School in 1941, Buck joined the National Guard to get something many teenagers didn't have much of in those days:

spending money. "You'll laugh at what I got. It was only twelve to thirteen dollars every three months, but that was spending money at that time. And I got my taste of military life."

Like most young men his age, he was about to get more than a taste. Prior to the Pearl Harbor attack, the National Guard was moved from individual state command and put under the wing of the federal government. "After that happened, they shipped us from Norfolk to Ft. Meade, Maryland, where we got more and more Army. We thought we'd only be in for one year and that we'd be coming home by early 1942. We thought we would be there to frolic and play and have a good time."

For most Americans the war that had broken out in Europe seemed far away. "All we knew was that there was an unrest in Europe in 1941, and that's all we knew. We were more concerned with our life right here in the U.S. But on December 7 we were on our way back to Ft. Meade from some training in North Carolina and that's when we heard about Pearl Harbor. We were then rerouted to Virginia Beach and they spread us out on the coastline for about a week as temporary guards because we didn't know what was coming at us next."

Thirty days later he was headed to England on a troop ship with 20,000 other American recruits. Just before leaving he married. It would be almost three years before he would see his bride again.

"I had my first taste of the war when arriving in England. When the British Navy came out to meet us just off Scotland, something went wrong. A British cruiser cut in front of us and we rammed it broadside, cutting it in half. Within two minutes both halves of it were sunk. I think most of them died, because we didn't stop for them. And that's something that hit us. We couldn't understand that there was a sinking ship out there and we didn't stop to pick up survivors. After a while we learned our ship was too valuable since we had 20,000 men on there. If we had stopped we would have been a perfect target for a German submarine. So the policy was to let the destroyers pick up who they could and we kept on going." Some 332 men died on that British cruiser, marking an inauspicious beginning to Williamson's division's arrival in Europe.

He was part of the almost two million Americans who would be stationed in Britain by D-Day. Overcrowding and nationality differences proved to be tense for both the Yanks and the Brits. The common lament British soldiers had for the Americans was, "Overpaid, oversexed, and over here." Yet, Williamson has fond memories of the United Kingdom. "The English people were great to us, although I'm sure we irritated them."

Williamson's 29th Division was one without a task for almost the first year it was overseas. In fact, Williamson's first few weeks in England were spent in a barn at a farmer's home until more organized arrangements could be made for the flood of Americans pouring onto the island. "At first, we did a lot of rebuilding for the English. Then, we did a lot of training."

The drills and exercises may have seemed pointless and unending, but they served as practice for the men and experimentation for the officers. "We didn't know it, but we were preparing for the invasion of France. We actually thought we were training to go to Africa until about January 1944 when the 29th was told that we were selected as a spearhead for the invasion."

By early 1944 the invasion of France had been on the drawing board for almost two years. The Allied leaders agreed that for Germany to be defeated a landing had to be made on the European mainland. Winston Churchill was the exception. He remained doubtful of the invasion's purpose and possible success until only a few months before it occurred. To achieve an eventual stronghold on the mainland meant hurling thousands of men and tons of supplies across open water into a well-fortified German line of defense. Amphibious landings had an infamous history of failure. The chances for disaster were great.

Political stress added to the pressures. If the invasion failed, it was feared that another attempt might not be feasible for months, perhaps longer. A failed crossing might also mean Hitler would have the flexibility to reinforce his decimated armies in Russia. Some historians believe it might have given Hitler enough leverage to broker a truce with the Russians. Hitler laid out these high stakes to his commanders in the West by saying, "The destruction of the enemy's landing attempt means more than a purely local decision on the Western Front. It is the sole decisive factor in the whole conduct of the war and hence its final result."

This point was fully understood by Hitler's foe, Gen. Dwight D. Eisenhower. Failure was not an option to Ike. To this end, he, his staff, and countless others worked tirelessly at planning. Operation Overlord, the code name for the invasion, would require a breadth of cooperation, training, diversion, supplies, and most of all courage, the likes of which the world had never seen.

Overlord called for the largest armada ever assembled. Ships and landing craft of all kinds were ordered and designed. Adaptations to tanks, vehicles, and weaponry were made. From new uniforms to more bombs, the needs seemed endless.

And that's where the might of American industrialism came in. It was up to factories across the country to not only physically get the troops across the English Channel, but also to arm them with the most and best equipment. In one of the truly amazing feats of the war, American factories, the "arsenal of democracy," churned out record numbers of ships, planes, and armament.

While the factories manufactured and the officers planned, the soldiers trained. Endlessly. Regardless of what tools they were given, the success of cracking the Atlantic Wall would ultimately come down to the men sent to do the job. Special schools were devised to prepare them for what they could expect. The 29th Division was the first to go through them.

One of Williamson's fellow 29ers recalls, "...loading and unloading landing craft, exiting, peeling off, quickly moving forward, crawling under barbed wire with live machine-gun fire just inches overhead and live explosions, strategically placed, detonated all around. We were schooled in the use of explosives. Satchel charges and bangalore torpedoes were excellent for blowing holes in barbed wire and neutralizing fortified bunkers. Bayonets were used to probe for hidden mines. Poison-gas drills, first aid, airplane and tank identification, use and detection of booby traps, and more gave us the confidence that we were ready. I believe our division was as competent to fight as any green outfit in history."

Williamson's job in the invasion was as part of a 105 howitzer crew in the 111th Field Artillery Battalion. It was a unit with a proud history, having fought in both the Civil War and World War I. As part of that unit, he worked closely with the infantry during training, learning how to support the troops that would be storming the beaches. "We made a number of dry runs by loading up in the Channel, then coming in to the beach for a rehearsal. We'd come in to a beach named Slapton Sands, trying all sorts of different methods of firing as the infantry moved in."

During one of the landing exercises at Slapton Sands, tragedy hit. German submarines slipped through the screen of destroyers and sank two landing craft and damaged six others. Some 749 men were killed and 300 were wounded even before the invasion began.

Despite the unending physical training, the daily artillery maneuvers, and the catastrophe at Slapton Sands, Williamson says morale was high. "Me personally, and I think many of my buddies had the same attitude, we were rehearsing for the big ballgame, and this was it. We really looked forward to it. We thought we were ready and that we could do the job."

June 5 was set as D-Day. It was on this day that the tide and moon conditions would satisfy the requests and requirements of the different branches involved in the attack. A minimum of a half-moon was needed as light for the channel crossing, and also for the paratroopers that would be dropped into France several hours before the beach invasion began. A low tide at dawn was also needed so the landing craft could come right up to the beach, then float away as the tide rose. The low tide would also help expose some of the obstacles and mines the Germans had placed beneath the high-water mark. Both of these would occur on June 5, with similar conditions on the 6th and 7th.

But June 5 brought with it high winds and driving rains, conditions which made it impossible to launch history's biggest invasion. The lead meteorologist assigned to Eisenhower's staff then promised a window of fairer weather on the 6th. He said the weather wouldn't be great, but it would be better. After weighing the odds of the weather versus delaying the operation possibly for another few weeks, Eisenhower simply said, "Let's go."

In his book *D-Day, June 6, 1944: The Climactic Battle of World War Two*, Stephen Ambrose summarizes the guillotine awaiting the attackers. *"..the GI hitting the beach in the first wave at Omaha would have to get through the minefields in the Channel without his LST blowing up, then get from ship to shore in a Higgins boat taking fire from inland batteries, then work his way through an obstacle-studded tidal flat of some 150 meters, crisscrossed by machine-gun and rifle fire, with big shells whistling by and mortars exploding all around, to find his first protection behind the shingle (either a thin, small line of smooth rocks or short sand dunes). There he would be caught in a triple crossfire - machine guns and heavy artillery from the sides, small arms from the front, mortars coming down from above."*

Heading into that firepower would be thousands of men, most of whom had never seen combat. One of those men was my grandfather. Like so many others, he was a green recruit being pushed into the greatest land defense system ever created.

Part of the Allies' plan to overcome the odds was a complex choreography of man and machine. Paratroopers would be dropped behind the main German defense six hours before the invasion. Their job was to disrupt German reinforcements that would be rushing to the front after the fighting started. At 5:20 A.M. the air bombardment would start. By 5:50 A.M. the naval bombardment would begin, lasting until 6:25, just five minutes before the troops hit the beach. The air and naval bombardment had an important two-pronged goal: destroy or immobilize the coastal guns or the Germans inside manning them, and to create craters in the sand to provide cover for the infantry. At 6:30 A.M., H-Hour, landing craft carrying tanks, infantry, engineers, demolition teams, artillery units, medical units, and support crews of all kinds, would come in, wave after wave, spaced only minutes apart. By 10:30 A.M., the bulk of the landing force was to either be on the beach or moving inland.

Landings would occur along five different beaches on the Normandy coastline, code named Omaha, Utah, Gold, Sword, and Juno. The Americans would land at Omaha and Utah, the British at Sword and Gold, the Canadians at Juno. Williamson was assigned to Omaha.

"The day before we left England to hit France, Gen. Cota told us, 'Things are going to go wrong. Some of you won't land at the right place. Some of you won't land at all. There will be complete confusion, but don't contribute to it.' And that's exactly what happened on D-Day. Everything went wrong," Williamson says.

During the predawn hours of June 6, an armada of 2,727 ships from New Zealand, Norway, Poland, France, Australia, Canada, Britain, Holland,

Belgium, South Africa, Greece, and the United States slipped away from ports all over southern England. On those ships was another 2,606 landing craft of all kinds, a total of 5,333 vessels. The ships gathered in the choppy, cold waters of the English Channel, then headed to the far shore.

"As soon as we pulled away from the docks they told us this was the invasion. This was not a dry run. Chaplains were holding service on the ships and they were feeding us well. We knew we were getting too much good treatment." Large troop and equipment transport ships stopped within three miles of the coast, then off-loaded the different infantry and artillery companies and regiments into smaller landing craft. Seas were choppy, winds were brisk, and vomit due to sea-sickness lined the floors of the landing craft.

Williamson's 111th Field Artillery Battalion was to land at 8:20 A.M. at Easy Red sector, Omaha Beach, one hour and fifty minutes after the first tanks and infantry hit the beach. Upon landing they were to immediately set up their guns for firing on inland positions. They never came close to fulfilling that mission. "For the 111th, we had a disaster. It all went wrong. We put each artillery piece in a DUKW ( pronounced "duck", it was an Army truck that had propellers for moving through water, yet could also operate at 50 mph on land). Then we put ammo, camouflage, and seven men in it as well. Then we put sandbags in the bottom of it to protect us from mines. Well, that overloaded the DUKW. So as soon as they came off the ship and hit the water, water started coming in over the sides. They had pumps on them, but they died within minutes, and they started sinking.

"When the first gun went down, we all started throwing stuff off those DUKWs. We threw off the camouflage net, half of the men, but they still kept going down, including the one I was on. Finally, the last two DUKWs that were heading in only had three men, no ammo and no sandbags. They started out pretty good, but then they, too, started bringing on water. One of them sank. The other DUKW just took off for the shore. He was going to make a run for it, and he actually was successful. But he was way off target and ended up in another division and they didn't give the gun back.

"Out of the twelve artillery pieces we had, eleven were on the bottom of the English Channel within fifty minutes. Our mission as artillery men was dead. So, we became stragglers. And that's where some of the good planning came in. They had these things called rhino ferries, and they were nothing more than steel tanks tied together with a motor on it. They picked us up and that's how we got in."

Much of today's public awareness of what happened that morning on Omaha Beach comes from the 1998 movie, *Saving Private Ryan*. The movie depicts carnage, chaos, and a sickening loss of life in it's portrayal of the landings. According to Williamson and many other D-Day veterans who saw the movie, it was actually much worse. Entire boat loads of men were decimated with machine gun fire as the landing ramp went down. Mortars and artillery blew men in half, ripped off arms and legs, and wreaked havoc on the boats coming in. The beach was littered with the dead and dying. Ninety-six percent of one company was either killed or wounded. The landing at Omaha was an immediate catastrophe.

By 10:30, when the landings were supposed to have been completed, the rhino ferry that had picked up Williamson was coming onto the beach. It was two hours past when he was supposed to have landed. "They had picked up a lot of soldiers. During the time from when we were picked up and when we got to the beach, it was just a question of survival. I've seen a lot of water in my day, but that's the first time I saw bullets splashing in the water. They carry a message. When you see a bullet splashing in water, you move, and you move fast. The machine guns were really hurting us. They just swept the water and the beach.

"As we came in, I saw a lot of people moving around, and a lot a bodies on the beach, and in the water. For some reason, the bodies in the water affected me more than those on the beach. I don't know why. And too many of us were just overloaded with equipment. We had what we called a Mae West (a circular life preserver that wrapped underneath the arms). Some of the Mae Wests slipped from their chest down to their waist. So that made their heads go down and their tails go up, so they drowned. After seeing what had happened, and what was happening to some of the others, I made sure my Mae West was up. I threw my helmet away because I didn't want the weight. I was figuring on finding a helmet once I got on the beach. I threw off as much dead weight as I could, but I kept my gas mask because it was in a canvas bag and it acted as a flotation.

"That's a wide, wide beach, but when I got there the tide had come in quite a bit, but I still had to run a good one hundred yards to get to the shelf, which guys were hiding behind. I'd run, then stop by just falling down. Those machine guns had a ripping sound. When you're laying down there, you can hear those bullets hitting the sand. In fact, when a bullet hits the sand, it splashes like water. So I looked around and figured there was no point in staying there. I don't know why I stopped. I guess it was because that's what the other guys were doing. So we'd run, then stop, run, then stop. Now we were a little fortunate in that by the time we got in there, there were enough troops scattered up and down the beach that the Germans had too many targets to fire at, so a lot of us got through. We didn't lose too many on the beach that got off our ferry. But some of the guys in my regiment did drown, or got killed on the beach.

"When I got up to the shelf, I began to see a few of my buddies from my outfit. I wouldn't say we were comfortable there, but we got some assurance from being with someone we knew. Misery loves company, I guess. Those of us who made it across scattered up and down the beach. We were very disorganized. We were there just waiting for somebody to tell us what to do. Our Lt. Col. Mullins did a wonderful job of getting us together. He was killed doing it. He was shot twice but just kept right on going until finally a sniper killed him. But he was the one that really pulled us together.

"There was a battle cry that went up and down the beach. The cry was, 'There are two kinds of people on this beach, the dead and those that are going to die! Let's get off!' It really did help to start us moving.

"Engineers began to slip up the shelf and blow holes in the barbed wire so men could try to go through it. Once in a while a brave guy would try to get over the shelf and the Germans would shoot him. But there was no just sitting around down there. That's where our leadership came in. They didn't let us sit long. They told us to get up there and get on the edge of that shelf, and if we saw someone to shoot them. Us artillery guys were trying to be infantrymen.

"When we didn't get off the beach that afternoon, and the sun started going down, we got scared. We actually thought the invasion had failed. Then we heard that some others had made a breakthrough and we had a little encouragement." In fact, by late afternoon there was a lot to be encouraged about compared to the carnage of the landing's first few hours. Between 11 A.M. and noon, a few small groups had made it over the shelf and were beginning to knock out some of the smaller machine gun nests. As the afternoon wore on, more and more German guns and soldiers were eliminated, thereby shrinking the killing zone on the beach below.

By late afternoon the troops at Easy Red, as well as at the other sectors on Omaha, had a toehold on the beach. German emplacements were being surrounded and slowly knocked out, yet preset mortars and artillery continued to rain down on the tightly packed troops and vehicles on the beach, adding to the number of dead and wounded. Throngs of boats packed with men and supplies cruised the clogged beach, looking for openings. Some hit mines, others were blown apart by German artillery.

By the end of June 6, 175,000 men had crossed the English Channel. Some never made it out of their boats. Others made it only a few frantic strokes in the water before either drowning or being cut down. And hundreds died even before the landings occurred as they parachuted behind enemy lines. Some 9,758 Allied soldiers (6,603 Americans) were either killed or wounded by day's end; 2,200 of those were at Omaha beach, many of whom within the first hour. For both Americans and Canadians, the first assault teams suffered almost a one-in-two chance of being killed or wounded.

As the German guns were slowly being silenced, Williamson spent the entire day crouched behind the shelter of the shelf, waiting for orders as to what his regiment should do next. Finally, by the next morning, with no resistance to harass them, Williamson's regiment and other infantry breached the shelf and made their way to a nearby church in the town of Vierville. "The Navy was bringing in all kinds of supplies and just dumping it on the beach. So, since we didn't have any artillery pieces, we helped bring some of it up to the church's courtyard. It was made into a kind of supply depot.

"Also, when we finally got off the beach, we captured a lot of their soldiers and found out that some of them were Polish, Hungarian, young kids and old men, so we began to think the Germans weren't so hot after all." As a matter of fact, many of the soldiers facing the Allies at Normandy had no ties to Germany at all, other than being forced by the Germans to fill their withering ranks. Conscripts from all over eastern Europe were brought out of slave-labor camps or occupied villages and forced to man guns, typically with a German officer standing behind them with a pistol pointed at their heads. Such was the German war machine in mid-1944.

Even so, Williamson and the rest of the Allies pouring into France were in for a long, bloody stretch in the hedgerow country into which they were moving. When the troops were told they would be fighting through hedgerows, they assumed they would be similar to the hedgerows they had seen in England: three to four feet high mounds that acted as small fences between pastures. That's not how they were in France. Their hedgerows were up to twelve feet tall with heavy hedges on top, and sturdy root systems anchored in the mounds. Williamson says, "It was the worst to fight in. It was excellent for defense, but awful for the offense. It offered such good protection for the Germans."

The Allies were mired in the maze and trap of the hedgerows for seven long weeks, gaining only a few hundred yards a day in some locations. Yet, armed once again with artillery, Williamson's regiment was finally able to do the work it had trained two years to do. "We worked very close with the infantry, sometimes within a hundred yards of the front line. As they advanced, so did we. Our forward observers would be up with them and direct our fire. Sometimes we'd shoot at buildings, sometimes at people. One gun would fire first and when it got to where the forward observer wanted it to be, then all the guns would come in on that one spot.

"And we were constantly worried about mines. They were all over the place. This was orchard and dairy country, so if you saw cattle in a field, you were safe to walk in it. But if there were no cattle, beware."

The Americans came into frequent contact with the French since they were now fighting in their fields and towns, and sleeping in their barns and homes. "At that time, we were told to trust no one. If we saw a French civilian, we'd feel sorry for him, but we had a policy of not trusting anybody. I felt so sorry for the French. We tore up their homes and killed their livestock, but they were still glad to see us. Now that I've been back over and have heard some of their stories, I wish I could have trusted them and been friendlier to them.

"But the American soldier, he's just different. Even if we didn't trust them or weren't allowed to, we'd give them a chocolate bar or a can of rations. But it wasn't the Prince and the Pauper situation at all. Life was miserable for us. The weather was terrible. And before we left England they gave us impregnated clothes which were wool pants and a shirt dipped in wax. They gave us those because they were worried about chemical warfare. Turns out that wasn't ever a real threat.

"It didn't breathe very well, and it was hot. We wore that same outfit for six weeks, without even a bath, sleeping on the ground. So, the living conditions were rough on us. But we did have plenty of food and ammo," which is something the Germans were quickly running out of in France.

"After we captured the town of St. Lo, the engineers would bring in these portable showers, which were big tanks of water with gas-powered heaters on them. They'd march us into one tent and we'd strip down. We'd go into the next tent and shower. In the third tent you picked up new clothes. I don't think they used our old clothes again since we had them on for six weeks."

By mid-August, almost two months after the landings, the Allies were finally able to break out of the Normandy countryside. By this point my grandfather had already had his "million-dollar wound" (troops often referred to wounds this way, because to them, going home was as good as having a million dollars). He was hit in Cherbourg, France, and was likely on his way back to England. But the 29th Division, including Williamson, continued to roll through France. After capturing the port city of Brest, France, in September, they rejoined the main thrust into Germany.

"The Germans put up a real good fight on their homeland and all along their two big rivers, the Ruhr and the Rhine. They were two big obstacles that had to be crossed. It was tough up there. It was kind of a shock when we got there, because after that nice ride through the rest of France, we got a little cocky. But when we got up to the German line, we thought, hey, this ballgame's not over yet ."

Far from it. Yet to come during the fall and early winter months would be the costly campaign of the Hurtgen Forest, the toll of the Battle of the Bulge, and the frustrating attacks along Germany's Siegfried Line. Fortunately for Williamson, the 29th Division was in Belgium, out of range of the more deadly battles that closed the war in Europe.

When the war finally ended in May, Williamson's regiment was ordered to deal with the growing and urgent problem of civilian and military refugees. "Our task was to round up displaced people. We just sent trucks up and down the road and we'd pick up people that were walking and looked like they were homeless. They didn't want to get in the truck, but we had to get them off the road so our supply vehicles could move through. Also, it was humane because they were starving.

"We set up a camp and housed and fed them with the expectation of getting them back to their homes. But we ran across a problem in the camp: You cannot mix nationalities. So, if you put, say, someone from the Netherlands in with someone from Germany, you had a fight. So we had to split them up into their own nationalities, especially the Russians.

"We found some Russians that had been in POW camps. They were extremely difficult to work with. You couldn't reason with them, you couldn't handle them. You'd have to almost shoot them to get them to do something. Finally one day, we picked up a Russian lieutenant. He was a young kid, maybe twenty-years-old. So we put him in charge and told him we'd give him all the vodka, whiskey, and food he wanted if he kept the other Russians in order. And it worked great. If we came across some cognac or some vodka, we'd give it to the lieutenant and he'd keep them in order. Fortunately, they left after a few weeks."

Williamson wasn't far behind. He was in one of the first groups sent home after the war. By the end of June 1945 he was on a bus to Norfolk to see the wife he hadn't seen in two years and nine months. When he walked through the door, he simply said, "I'm home."

In 1945, Buck Williamson couldn't wait to get back home. Nowadays, he can't wait to go back to France. In 1994, he crossed the Atlantic again, this time by plane, to join four hundred other members from the 29th Division to honor the 50th Anniversary of D-Day. The following year he went back to Normandy again, except this time with veteran local news anchor Jim Kincaid, who was doing a story on local D-Day veterans. Williamson also paid homage at the monuments and cemeteries in Normandy in 1997 and 1999.

"It's not emotional for me when I see the monument that's there for us at Vierville. I can read it and look all around and it doesn't affect me. But when a Frenchman comes up to me and thanks me, it kind of hits me. They are very, very grateful."

He wishes the folks back home would be as grateful. "A lot of people don't seem to be interested, and that's bothersome. But after the 50th Anniversary, and all the publicity it received, it sort of woke some people up. I think we realize more and more now of how important the values are that we have around us, and the necessity to protect those values. I think World War II was a giant example of that. In everyday life we have our little values that we have to learn to protect. They're not going to stay with us if we don't protect and fight for them."

# D-DAY

## PART II

## ROCCO RUSSO

1943

2000

Four hours before Buck Williamson stumbled onto Omaha Beach, the first wave of men tried to exit their landing craft. Some were killed the instant the ramp went down, others after having spent only a few seconds in the chest-deep water. Within minutes, one entire company was annihilated, others cut in half. The first wave was a murderous chaos. Rocco Russo was a part of it.

Like Williamson, Rocco Russo was born in Norfolk. He attended Trinity High School, now closed for many years. "I graduated from high school on June 1, 1943, and received my notice from the President of the United States that I was being drafted. And on June 24 three of my friends and a whole bunch of other people went up to Richmond to take our physicals. That was also our day of induction." Russo says he was excited about going into the Army, "I guess because Norfolk was a Navy town, and the Army was going to be something different. I remember my dad told me, 'Son, don't do anything to try to win a medal. You just do whatever you have to do.'"

After a few days back home in Norfolk to say his goodbyes, Russo spent the next seventeen weeks at Camp Croft, South Carolina, for infantry replacement training. By early 1944 he was on a troop ship with thousands of other young men, headed for England to prepare for the invasion of France.

He was assigned to Williamson's 29th Division, and placed in the 116th Regiment, F Company. It was tagged as one of the companies that would lead the charge across the Channel.

"The first day that I joined F Company we were in Plymouth, England. We went into a gymnasium and the colonel said, 'I want to welcome you to the 116th Regiment, F Company. This is a company that will land in the first wave of the invasion.' And then he stopped. Then he said, 'If you're thinking of a way of getting out of it, forget about it. There isn't any way.' But I wasn't thinking about getting out of it. I figured I was in the infantry, I was a soldier, I was there to fight a battle, and I was going to be ready. Maybe if I wasn't so naive I would've been scared to death.

"The first person I ran into who was really upset about it was eight years older than I was. He was married and had a baby son. He was sure he was going to get killed on the beach. I kept telling him, 'Tony, we're not going to get killed. We're going to be in good shape.' They told us about the support we were going to get from the Air Corps, and the support from the Navy ships, so I really did think we would be O.K. But things were worse on Omaha Beach than we ever imagined."

Russo and the rest of the 29th continued their grueling, unending preparations for Operation Overlord during the spring of 1944. By early May, a few weeks before the invasion, the mass transport of men and materiel to the southern coast of England was underway. Secrecy was of the utmost concern, so after the men were positioned in their marshalling areas, no one was allowed to leave or enter the fenced camps.

"About three of four days before June 5, when D-Day was supposed to be, we moved into the marshalling areas. They told us right away that this was the real thing, because each time we went in for the practice invasion, we didn't know if it was real or not. They told us that Gen. Patton was coming the next day to speak to us, so I got all excited, because even at that time Gen. Patton was a legend. I thought if I had to be like anybody in the Army it would be like Old Blood and Guts Patton.

"So right after they told us, I talked to two of my buddies and said, 'Why don't we go on over to the field where he's going to be and pick out a place to sit when we go over there tomorrow. So the next day we got there early enough that I could have reached out and touched him.

"What he told us was, 'Why have you been selected to be in the first wave? Because you're the best soldiers in the Army. In the whole world.' Well I thought, you know, I've only been in the Army for eleven months, I haven't yet been in combat, but coming from him it sounded great. The next thing he told us was, 'People talk about giving their lives for their country. Don't you even consider giving your life for your country. You make that other son of a bitch give his life for his country! You'll make a hero out of him when they get his body back in Berlin.' He told it to us the way we wanted to hear it."

On the night of June 5, 1944, nearly 175,000 Allied troops were on board their transport ships heading to the far shore. The weather was terrible. Wind and waves whipped the Channel into a dangerous mess, erasing the possibility of the invasion that was supposed to occur the next morning. "We were supposed to have been awakened at 11 P.M. the night of the 4th. Apparently by that time they had decided not to go because of the bad weather. So when we woke up on the morning of the 5th, we woke up to Eisenhower's voice telling us the invasion had been postponed. We thought, 'Good, we can shoot some more crap.'

"The biggest entertainment we had in my outfit was shooting crap. That's what we did on the 5th. The funny thing is, my buddy and I had pooled our money and realized we had won $1,600! I don't know what we thought we'd do with $1,600 once we got into combat. But we had a soldier's deposit that we could put our money in, and that's what we did."

By the night of June 5, Eisenhower's staff meteorologist promised a brief clearing on the 6th. After some bickering between the different military branches on the idea of another postponement, which likely would have been for another two weeks, Eisenhower's verdict was to go. The airborne units were dispatched, the Navy began to move into place, and the troop ships prepared to unload their human freight onto hundreds of smaller landing craft.

"That night of the 5th they called us down for chow, but my friend Tony, the one who was sure he was going to get killed, was so down in the dumps that I decided to just stay with him, so we didn't go eat.

"About 1 A.M. they came in and said, 'We got some good news for you. Instead of going down the rope ladder into the LCVP (landing craft), we're going to load you directly into the LCVP, pick you up with a crane, and lower you over the side of the ship into the Channel. That way you won't have to worry about the rope breaking or falling.' I was elated, because we were really loaded down. I weighed 148 pounds on D-Day, but I was carrying an 80 pound pack.

"So we got on the boat, they picked us up, they moved us over to the side, but they didn't move us over far enough to clear the ship. So when they started lowering us into the Channel, the two scraped sides and we started tilting. And boy, if we had been dumped into the water, I'm sure we would have drowned. We all screamed. They came over to see what was wrong, saw what the problem was, moved the crane over a little, then lowered us down."

All over the English Channel, in the dark of night without the aid of moonlight, throngs of landing craft motored around to gather in their proper groups according to the sector of the beach on which they were to land. Russo's group was DR 1, meaning Dog Red sector, boat 1. It is interesting to note that according to Russo's wife, the number on Russo's boat is the same number that appears on the boat in which Tom Hanks is aboard in *Saving Private Ryan*.

"We had no idea how many ships were out there because it was pitch black. This was just after 1 A.M., but we weren't supposed to hit the beach until 6:30, so we were taking our time getting in. We were in that LCVP for five-and-a-half hours, and the waves and the spray were terrible. It was really uncomfortable. Then people started getting seasick. I remember my buddy was seasick and he threw up on me, and that made me get sick, and then I started throwing up."

As the troops moved in, one of the great failures of the invasion was taking place. The swarm of B-17s and B-26s that was to pulverize the beachhead dropped most of its bombs well behind the German lines due to cloud cover and intense antiaircraft flak. The Army Air Corps that was supposed to strafe the beaches and knock out additional gun emplacements made only a dent due to the low cloud ceiling. The naval bombardment, which was to take out the larger guns, performed well in its given mission, yet did little to affect the Germans sitting in their trenches watching the tiny landing craft come toward them. The green bluff along the beach should have been brown and in flames by the time the infantry got there. The church spires that had been used as landmarks for reconnaissance purposes were supposed to have been demolished. Craters from bombs were supposed to have dotted the beach, acting as foxholes in which the troops could take cover. But as the men peered over the sides of their craft, their stomachs sank as they saw a beach that was quiet and virtually untouched.

At 6:25 A.M. all bombardment stopped and the job was turned over to the men who had trained months for this one day. Russo's F Company was supposed to land abreast with G Company, but due to the strong tide and choppy seas, G Company drifted far left, putting them nearly on top of F Company. With the two groups coming in tightly together instead of spread out, the Germans were able to concentrate their fire on them. It was a common scene up and down Omaha Beach.

"When we landed, we could hear the machine gun bullets hitting the ramp, and the ramp wouldn't go down. Our lieutenant yelled at the sergeant, 'Sergeant, what do we do now?' The sergeant told him he'd have to go over the side. So we gave the lieutenant a boost up the side of the boat, and when he was about ready to jump over, finally the ramp went down. The lieutenant and sergeant were scheduled to go down first and split off to different sides. I was to go left, behind the sergeant."

Russo's boat was relatively lucky compared to some of the others. They were able to avoid the underwater mines and the incoming shells, allowing the thirty-four men to exit their LCVP generally as planned. "But, as soon as I got in the water, I fell in all the way up to my neck, but I was able to recover. Then it was just a matter of getting to the beach because there was a lot of machine gun fire coming at us.

"When we finally got to the beach we looked for the pillboxes we had been told were supposed to be there. We were going to use our bazooka against those. My friend, Louis Simmons, was the gunner on our bazooka, and he wanted to fire it up at the hills, but I told him I didn't think we should do that since we couldn't see anything. The Germans used smokeless powder, so whatever they were firing you couldn't see where it was coming from at all. But Simmons just wanted to fire that gun. So we got up on our knees, fired two shells, then hit the sand again. I told him, 'Louis, I don't know about you, but I'm not going to fire any more until we can get up to a place where we can do some good. I'm going to get up to that seawall."

That seawall was 400 yards away. It was a six to eight foot manmade wall that prefaced a larger bluff behind the seawall. To get there meant crossing a killing zone swept by machine gun bullets, pounded by mortars, and rigged with mines. Men were being killed by the dozens trying to reach the sliver of protection that wall offered.

"One thing I did see when Simmons and I were lying there on the sand after we had fired those two shells, was I looked over to my right, and Sgt. John Cooney was lying there. He was a real good friend of mine. We used to go to mass together in England along with my friend Tony. His head had dropped forward, and his helmet had fallen upside down on the beach. He kind of had his head resting on his chin. And about that time, a shell landed close to him, and he didn't move. He was dead. That was the first dead soldier I saw."

Russo would see many more. Only fifteen minutes into the invasion, dead bodies, some dismembered, littered a very short stretch of beach. Dozens floated in the water, swaying in the incoming tide. Many of those still lucky to be alive were huddled, frozen still, behind any cover they could find: a sunken tank, a German obstacle, or the shingle of rocks that lined parts of the beach. But the only feature that offered any real protection was the distant seawall. Russo and Simmons made a run for it.

"I told Simmons, 'When there's nobody running, I'm going to get up and start running, and you get up with me. And then if we hear the German machine gun firing, we'll know they were firing at us because we'll be the only ones up and running. That'll tell us to get down. Then we'll do the same thing again.' We probably did that eight to ten times, and that's how we got up to the seawall. It probably took about thirty minutes, but we made it.

The seawall's protection was deceptive. The Germans knew the invaders would run for the wall, so they had pre-sighted their heavy artillery and mortars along the top of it. "Once we got up to the seawall, we dug a little bit of a hole to give us a little more protection. Sgt. Ryan told us, 'Look, we have

M-1 rifles, and we need to clean them because they'll jam from the saltwater and sand. So we all cleaned our rifles. I put mine just above where my hole was, and all of a sudden an 88 shell came in and we all ducked.

"When I came up I happened to look down, and there was a big hunk of meat in my lap. It had hit my assault jacket, and I had blood all the way down me. I said, 'Sergeant Ryan, look!' He looked at me and said, 'Is that from you?' I said, 'I don't know! I really don't know, but I think it's not.' I found out it was from a guy who had lost his leg, and it had hit me. Boy, what a scary thing."

By 8:30 A.M., with the first few waves in shambles and reduced to half their fighting strength, all landings of supplies and men were stopped. The beach was backed up with vehicles and men that had nowhere to go, so the incoming boats simply turned around, headed back, then milled around in circles waiting for things to clear. No more landings meant the men still alive would have to go it alone, without the support of more troops or more firepower.

Despite the futility of this situation, leadership took over. Brave individuals stepped forward and took command, from buck privates to generals. They led their men, their buddies, over the seawall and up toward the bluff that housed the German trenches. Russo recalls, "We were still taking a beating from the 88s and the mortars, but we decided with Ryan to get the combat engineers to clear some of the mines. Once they cleared the mines along the seawall, we were able to move along that cleared path to the higher bluff.

"In that bluff, what the German machine gunners did was, they were inside a trench, and they had mirrors set up so they wouldn't have to stick their heads up above the top of the trench. A German could look at those mirrors to see who to shoot at, and he didn't even have to be at his machine gun because some of them had a piece of cable that they pulled to activate the trigger. They weren't even coming close to being hit."

With the aid of big guns from naval destroyers that had moved in dangerously close to shore, the slowly-advancing GIs were beginning to get some help. "I figured if we could get off the beach and up on the bluff, others could do it, too. But once we got up there, we ran into the German machine guns again. We were fortunate, though. We destroyed two of those machine guns in one of those trenches with our bazooka. Oh, Simmons and I were elated. Then we saw a man running over to us and he said, 'Thank you, son!' We looked at his shoulder, and he was a brigadier general, Gen. Cota. In the movie, *The Longest Day*, Robert Mitchum played the part of Gen. Cota. He told us to stick with him and jokingly said, 'I think I'd make a pretty good squad leader,' which normally would just be a sergeant."

By early to mid-afternoon the bottleneck at the beach was thinning somewhat, and small groups of men were beginning to make their way off the beach. They were still being plunged with bullets and artillery, but sheer numbers were starting to overwhelm the Germans.

"Later that day we made it into a small village and started to liberate it. There were two machine guns inside of a house and we knocked those out, too. Oh, Gen. Cota was pleased. He was pleased with us. Before it got dark he took us over to a cemetery by a road. He said, 'I want you to dig a two-man foxhole between these two graves. If the Germans send tanks up this road, it'll be up to you to stop the tanks.' He was as naive as we were. Knocking out those machine guns was easy, but it was tough to knock out one of those big German Tiger tanks. The only way really was to knock the track off. So we spent the night in that cemetery, and the Germans never sent any tanks. It was a quiet night where we were."

At the end of June 6, F Company was scattered, disorganized, and nearly half of its men were dead or wounded. That morning they had landed with 187 men and officers. By nightfall, 26 were dead and 53 were wounded.

Russo's father, who had implored him to try not to win any metals, called a high-ranking military friend of his when he learned that Rocco's company was involved in the invasion. He asked, "Do you have anything on my son? Did he win any medals?" And as a matter of fact he had. F Company was awarded the Presidential Unit Citation, and Rocco had earned his combat infantry badge.

When asked how well the movie *Saving Private Ryan* portrayed what he went through on Omaha Beach, Russo says, "The first 20-25 minutes of the movie were very realistic. After that, it was a bit of Hollywood. And one thing it lacked, was they didn't even mention the hedgerows. The hedgerows were terrible. We lost more people in the hedgerows than we lost on D-Day. Every day in the hedgerows was like another D-Day. Just terrible."

And what about Russo's friend Tony, the one who was convinced he was going to get killed on the beach? "Tony was not killed on D-Day. At the end of each day after that, we'd look each other up. On July 12, he was killed in the hedgerows. I was digging a slit trench with a buddy of mine, and someone came over and said, 'Rocco, I've got some bad news for you. Tony's been killed.' I asked if he could take me to him, and we went over to where he was. He was lying on his stomach. We turned him over, and he had been shot from shoulder to shoulder with a German machine gun. Eventually, his wife had him buried back home."

As bands of men continued to mop up the beach defenses, Russo and what was left of F Company regrouped on June 9. As he walked back along the sea-wall to rejoin his buddies, he saw the death left from three days before. "That's when we saw all the bodies. It was just terrible. You looked at them and thought, 'Why not me?'" That's a question he would have to ask himself time and time again in the upcoming weeks.

As the 29th Division suffered through the hedgerows that lie a few miles inland, lessons were learned the hard way. "There was no way to get through those hedgerows, so at one time we were blowing a hole through them so the tank that was supporting us could go through. But as soon as they started

116

going through the hole, with all that black smoke from the explosion, the Germans would zero in on the smoke and knock out the tank. So finally, this enlisted man who was a mechanic suggested that they put a blade on the front of the tank to push its way through. From then on, we were successful in the hedgerows. Before that, it was just murder."

Louis Simmons and Rocco Russo had been fighting side by side for ten days, seven of those in the hedgerows. "Simmons and I knocked out a German tank on our tenth day by knocking off its track. There was another tank close by, and he turned his turret around with the fifty-caliber machine gun. One bullet killed Simmons, and one bullet destroyed the bazooka. I was just behind him by only two or three feet. He was killed instantly. We both ducked down, and I don't know how they missed me.

"For some reason, I blocked that out for a lot of years. I never did tell my wife about Simmons until we went back there for the 50th Anniversary of D-Day in 1994."

Shortly after, Russo was transferred to a mortar crew. Company F continued to take high casualties, especially among the officers. By mid-June, none were left. Four had been killed, three were wounded. In fact, the 29th Division, which F Company was in, suffered one of the highest casualty rates of all divisions in the U.S. military.

Despite the losses, Russo says there was still an air of bravado in their actions. "There were so many things that we did that were sometimes cocky. But we were beginning to need a little bit of that. I remember one day when I was the gunner of the mortar, we were behind a hedgerow. Usually, when we took a hedgerow, the Germans would leave. They'd either be captured, be killed, or move back a hedgerow. But for some reason a group of them didn't. So when we got up to the hedgerow we could hear them talking on the other side, just five to six feet away. There must have been ten or twelve of them.

"So I got my squad leader, Buddy, and I said, 'Buddy, you know what I'd like to do? I'd like to fire the mortar when it's almost straight up and down, and just move it a tad, and fire a couple of shells to try to hit those Germans.' What a tad was to me was when you moved it, and you knew that you moved it, but you couldn't tell that you moved it. Anyhow, I said, 'Before I fire, you guys move down the hedgerow in case this thing comes down on our side. And then as soon as I drop a shell in, I'll run down there so I won't get hit, and we'll see what happens.' So I fired one shell, and do you know, it knocked out those Germans. Killed every one of them. Now, we had a guy who was doing some spotting for us. And in 1995 I was at his house in South Boston, Virginia. We were reminiscing about that, and he said, "Rocco, that shell hit the steel helmet of one of those German soldiers. It landed right in the middle of them."

And so it went until August 4, 1944, when Russo almost met the same fate as his friends Tony and Louis.

"We were trying to get to the town of Vier, and we were still in the hedgerows. When you're in the infantry, every time you stopped, you started digging a hole, because you might be there all night, or maybe you wouldn't. So, Buddy, Marty, and I dug our holes. Then we set up our mortar and we were ready to go back to our hole and all of a sudden a shell came in, and I saw it hit just three feet in front of me. The shell hit all of us.

"It killed one guy, Buddy had a bad chest wound, Marty had a bad arm wound, and I had a bad stomach wound. I didn't know I was even wounded. So I told the other guys to try to run back to an aid station that I had seen back a ways. Then I started to get up, and I couldn't because it hurt so much. I pulled my pants down and my shirt up, and I had a small hole that wasn't bleeding in my lower abdomen. It was a small piece of shrapnel. But we all three made it back to the aid station, even with those terrible wounds. It's a wonder we didn't go into shock."

When Russo arrived for help, he was given his shot or morphine. "Morphine takes about twenty minutes to kick in, and after that it takes away all the pain." Whoever injected the morphine would write with a pen on the wounded soldier's forehead what time and what day the morphine was given so as to avoid an overdose. Two injections at one time could be fatal. He was then transferred farther back to a more sophisticated aid station where he was immediately given a blood transfusion. After finally arriving in a field hospital in Le Havre, France, Russo went quickly into surgery where the doctor found seven puncture wounds in his intestines.

He spent the next fifteen days in post-op, laying under a big, open tent with dozens of other men. One of the things that comes to mind when he thinks back on those fifteen days is listening to Bing Crosby and other famous singers of the time on a radio that had been set up for the wounded.

Russo was eventually shipped to a large hospital in England. "I used to complain about how they passed out the purple hearts. They had this shopping cart with two medics, and it was loaded with purple hearts. And as they walked past the bed they'd toss one on it. I said, 'Damn, aren't you even going to pin it on me?' They said, 'We don't have time for that.' When we went back in 1994, the Governor of Normandy pinned a beautiful gold medal on each one of us (including Buck Williamson). I said, 'Governor, I appreciate that. That's the first medal anyone has ever pinned on me other than myself. He smiled at me and just said, 'You're welcome.'"

Although Russo was listed as an E grade, the lowest grade a wounded man could receive, he eventually recovered enough to venture out into Exeter, England. "A friend of mine, who was wounded when jumping into France, and I used to go into pubs whenever we could sneak out of the hospital, which was tough because of the physical grade we were in. Sometimes the MPs would see us out and ask us where we were going because we didn't have passes. They'd say, 'That's alright. Which pub do you want to go to? We'll take you there, and when it closes we'll pick you up and take you back.' It was wonderful! "But we did have a problem with the British Marines. They had come back from the Pacific and they really gave us a hard time. Every time we'd go into town they'd come over and pick a fight with the wounded from the hospital. So we put a bug in the big boss's ear over at the 82nd Airborne Division Headquarters that we needed some help. The guy said he'd take care of it, and they went in there and beat the heck out of all those British Marines. Just beat them up terribly!"

Russo thought he was headed back home. When he was shipped to England the doctors even told him he was. He wrote his mom and dad to tell them he'd be back home in Norfolk for Christmas. But the Battle of the Bulge in December of 1944 changed all that. "They lost so many guys that they needed replacements. So they ended up sending me back to a headquarters artillery group where they made a radio operator out of me."

During the spring of 1945 the Allies were pushing strongly through western Germany toward Berlin. It was at this time that one of the Nazis' most horrific atrocities was finally uncovered. "On April 29, 1945, we were attached to the 42nd Infantry Division when they liberated the Dachau concentration camp. We were getting ready to eat chow that night, and the colonel came out and said, 'If you guys don't know why you're fighting this war, I'm going to show you.'

"I had never heard of a concentration camp and we had no idea what had been going on. They had to explain it to us. When we got to within a mile of Dachau, the stench was just unbearable. We went through the camp and all we saw were dead bodies. There were boxcars all around the camp full of dead bodies. Some 32,000 prisoners were liberated. Had we been there two days sooner, maybe we could have liberated 64,000. But the reverse of that is had we been there two days later we wouldn't have liberated any because those Nazi bastards would have murdered them all.

"In the two-hour period before we got there, the Army let the prisoners go, and they were afraid the Jews were going to get hurt. So they put them behind some fences and sent some American doctors to start looking at them individually. They were just skin and bones."

Like most veterans who fought in Europe, Russo has found it in his heart to forgive his enemy. "When I first came home, if anyone would have suggested I buy a Mercedes Benz, I would have said no. But I started thinking about it and thought that the bulk of the Germans were fighting for their country just like I was fighting for mine. We reached a point where we had to kill them or they would have killed us. One of the things we would say when we killed a German was, 'Better thee than me.' But now, I think we've become great allies."

Rocco Russo didn't talk about what he had seen or been through after he came home. He didn't talk about his friends who had been killed or the

Germans he had killed. "I didn't do a lot of talking about it until 1994 when they had the 50th Anniversary. Before then, I would talk a little about some of the funny things that had happened over there, but that was about it. But when we went back to France and started mingling with the French people, they were just elated with us. They were so nice to us. I think a lot of guys started opening up after that."

At the insistence of his children, Russo has put down on paper his thoughts and memories from World War II. He wants them to know what he went through, and what others who didn't make it back went through. He even does a few speaking engagements, trying to encapsulate in mere words the terror on Omaha Beach, the grind of the hedgerows, the pain of hot shrapnel, and the shock of seeing the grim results of Nazi hatred. It was the worst that war had to offer.

### A Memorial Long Overdue

Rocco Russo made a pilgrimage to Bedford, Virginia, on Memorial Day, 2000. Bedford, with a population of only 3,200 in 1944, was the home of Company A of the 116th Regiment. It was among the first to hit Omaha Beach. Of the company's 170 soldiers in the first assault wave, 91 men died, 64 were wounded, and only 15 were able to continue fighting. Of the 35 young men from Bedford, 19 died in the invasion's first fifteen minutes, and two more died later that day. Almost an entire generation of Bedford residents was erased.

Historians say the 21 deaths from the Town of Bedford on D-Day were the highest per-capita loss from any single community in our country. Because Bedford symbolizes the sacrifices that were made not only across the country, but also across the world that day, the small town of now 6,200 is the chosen site for The National D-Day Memorial.

The 88-acre site, with a view of the Blue Ridge Mountains, will feature a granite arch monument overlooking reflecting pools. A key feature of the memorial will be the Education Center that will house an auditorium and education work stations, in addition to research and archival work stations.

John Slaughter, chairman of The National D-Day Memorial Foundation, a Roanoke resident, and a D-Day veteran, states the importance of the Memorial as this: "The only memorial truly honoring the valor, fidelity, and sacrifice of the Allied Armed Forces on D-Day, June 6, 1944 - indeed, honoring any who lost their youth, blood, life in war - is one that tirelessly promotes vigilance and justice in the interest of global peace."

*Rocco Russo passed away in February 2001.

1942                  2000

A single afternoon in 1932 changed the course of Mary Damon's life. At 18 years old, Mary was nearing graduation from high school and was planning to attend business school. That was before she saved her neighbor's life.

"One of the men and his wife were having problems," recalls Mary. "He was drunk and wanted to get into their house, so he put his fist through the glass door in the kitchen and cut his wrist. One of the daughters came over and said, 'Mary, please come over! Dad cut his hand and blood is all over the place!' So I went over and saw that blood was just squirting out of one of his arteries. I just put my hand on it and everything stopped. Apparently, I saved the man's life."

On that day, Mary Damon learned that she was destined to be a nurse. What she did not know was that the discovery would take her to the front lines of a war soon to rage in Europe.

Mary Damon, born Mary Fedor, spent the first five years of her life surrounded by war. She was born an American citizen in the Slovakian province of Austria-Hungary in March 1914, only six months before that country became embroiled in what was then called the Great War (by World War II it was referred to as World War I). After the war started it became impossible to leave Europe safely. Mary, her older brother, and her mother were forced to live the next five years in the middle of the Great War, with Mary spending much of her time hiding in an underground potato cellar.

Finally in 1920 the family was able to return home to Braddock, Pennsylvania. "We were very well off because my father and uncle had a butcher and grocery shop. I had oodles of little friends because they always got something to eat when they came over to visit me. We even had a gypsy community in Braddock and they'd come over to our backyard and play Hungarian and Slovak music and my dad would feed them."

Mary spent her teenage years in Braddock growing up in relative comfort while depression gripped the country. Her father had decided that she would attend business school after high school. "In those days, women could vote, but you were still under the thumb of the family." But saving a man's life empowered daughter Mary to choose her own path.

"After that incident with the neighbor, our family doctor, Dr. Polk, said, 'Mary, you know what I want you to do? I want you to be a nurse.' Well, I had been planning to go to business school, but I thought about it and thought about it and decided that it would be a good challenge. So that's how I got into nursing."

Damon was accepted to the Columbia Hospital School of Nursing in Williamsburg, Pennsylvania. After graduating in 1937, her supervisor recommended her for post-graduate courses because Damon showed promise as a surgical nurse. She then spent the next six months in Chicago for specialized training in operating room technique. She was on her way to being an operating-room supervisor, a desired and lucrative position.

By 1939 Damon had her first full-time job as a nurse. "I took a job as an assistant operating room supervisor in Alabama because they paid the most. They gave me $75 per month, plus full maintenance." It was good pay for a woman in a country that was racked by economic depression.

"One night we were listening to the radio and heard that war was declared. I told my roommate, 'I think I'm going to join.' She asked why I wanted to do that and I said, 'I'm sure they'll be needing surgical nurses.' A little later I read in the paper they did need nurses, so I went down and signed up. I was young and I had a lot of moxie."

When Pearl Harbor was bombed there were only 1,000 nurses enlisted in the Army Nurse Corps. In the few days following the attack, as hundreds of casualties poured into hospitals in Hawaii, it was apparent that medical facilities were dismally understaffed. Following a campaign blitz to bring in more nurses, the number of Army nurses grew to 12,000 within six months.

As part of that rush to serve, Damon was sent to Camp Rucker, Alabama, for four weeks of Army basic training. Initially, nurse recruits spent most of their time training men to become surgical corpsmen. "I taught them how to set up for surgery and I taught them the sterile technique and also how to give the instruments to the doctor. It was stuff that was absolutely necessary."

It may have been necessary but it wasn't enough for a girl with "moxie." Damon decided that she wanted to be in the middle of the action and opted to go on training maneuvers with the men. "We came to help the boys in any way we could. So I decided I wanted to be out there with them to see what I could do."

Damon says that despite the newness of their presence, women were there to help the men, not distract them. "We were too busy with our own jobs. We didn't have time for foolishness between us and the boys. I've thought about that many times. We had a lot of male friends, but nothing was done beyond friendship. There was dating, but it was clean dating. There was none of this looking at someone and saying, 'Come on, let's go to bed' like there is nowadays."

Women on the battlefield wasn't the only experiment going on during the early days of the war. There was a new drug that showed great promise in treating infections. It had already proven helpful in treating venereal diseases, and it was hoped that it could be used on the battlefield to stave off infections in wounds. This new wonder drug was called penicillin. "At the time, we were still experimenting with it. There were a lot of boys with syphilis, and they wanted that penicillin. I felt sorry for every boy I gave a shot to because the needles were big and you had to give them a lot of fluid. It was very painful. I didn't mind giving shots, but I wasn't sure about the penicillin shots since it was still experimental. But it did help the boys."

The experiment of nurses landing in an invasion force began in November of 1942. Off the coast of North Africa, nurses waded ashore with the troops in Operation Torch. Huddled behind sand dunes, they dodged sniper fire until they were finally able to get to work in a vacant building. It was a scene that would be repeated time and time again in the upcoming months.

The tremendous demands for manpower and supplies for the upcoming invasion of France were growing by early 1944. To deal with the glut of expected casualties, the number of surgical groups was increased and sent to England. Damon was part of one of those groups. She boarded a troop ship and headed for England in March 1944. "We were wondering if we were going to get torpedoed. We had to keep everything ready. You slept for eight hours, then had to be on the deck for the rest of the time because someone else was using your bed."

While the months leading up to D-Day were marked by endless training for the soldiers, it was mostly a waiting period for the nurses. They were given no active work, and spent much of their time giving tours of American medical facilities and explaining American surgical techniques.

Even though Damon was still on the English side of the Channel, the Germans had developed a new weapon that wreaked havoc through destruction and fear. "You'd go to bed and the next thing you knew you were hearing something go VROOM! They were the buzz bombs the Germans were sending in. Thank goodness I heard that noise, because if you didn't hear it, you had had it. You just hoped that wherever it landed it didn't kill many people. It was very terrorizing."

Approximately one month before D-Day, a letter went out to hospital units asking for nurse volunteers to follow the invasion force into France. They would be a part of surgical units stationed right behind the front lines. The job would be dangerous, the odds unknown. It was just what Mary Damon had in mind.

Unlike the soldiers, nurses and doctors were given no pep talks before heading into Hitler's Atlantic Wall. But Damon and a few other nurses sneaked a listen to what was surely a speech meant for no woman's ears. "A bunch of us went into the high weeds to listen to Gen. Patton's pep talk that he was giving to the boys. Women weren't allowed to listen, so we hid down on our bellies. I didn't hear a thing that sounded like advice, but it was full of words that I can't use myself. I mean every other word!"

Although there were combat medics and a few surgeons who landed or parachuted in on D-Day, most of the medical staff was held back for two days after the landing. A bad storm in the Channel delayed their arrival until the third day. Damon says that while on their way over to France they had no idea how the fighting had gone and were unsure of what would happen to them. She simply remembers thinking, "If the boys can go across, why can't I?"

On June 9, Damon's 3rd Auxiliary Surgical Group Team landed at Omaha Beach. The section of beach she landed on was clear, showing no signs of the bloodletting that occurred just three days prior. She remembers no obstacles, no burning vehicles, yet does recall bodies in temporary graves. Only later would Damon learn the price that had been paid there.

Doctors, nurses, and corpsmen were loaded into trucks, jeeps, and ambulances and taken immediately toward the front line. "At first, about the only thing we saw lying dead were animals. All of the boys had been taken care of or buried. But as we were driving in, we saw some of the dead paratroopers still dangling in the trees. Those were the first dead bodies we saw. We had prepared ourselves to see a lot more." She soon would.

Damon's group immediately launched into the task of setting up their field hospital just outside the town of Carentan, France, only five to seven miles inland. The wounded and dying were already waiting there for help.

Damon's surgical group was assigned to a field hospital, which meant they were usually only one to two miles from the front line. It was the first stop for the casualties being brought in by jeep, ambulance, stretcher, or on the back of a buddy. Most had already been given stop-gap care and a stick of morphine by a medic at the front. Each field hospital could handle 75 to 150 patients.

As the wounded men were carried in, they were immediately evaluated by doctors to see what needed to be done. Those that were stable enough for travel were sent farther back to larger station hospitals. Eventually they would be sent to England to a larger, general hospital. Men who needed surgery but were too weak for an immediate operation and could not travel were sent to the shock ward. Soldiers who could handle immediate surgery were sent into tents like Mary Damon's.

"Our group took care of mostly sucking chest wounds, abdominal wounds, or amputations that were started in the field by a medic and needed to be finished and cleaned. We had two surgery tables going, and I was usually the floating nurse between the two, making sure the surgeons always had all the supplies they needed."

In that tent, Damon saw what hot metal from bullets and shells can do to the human body. "It tears everything apart. It just mutilates the body. I can't explain it. Shreds of skin, shreds of bone, just hanging loose. We'd spend hours seeing if we could put boys back together. Sometimes we were fortunate, but three-fourths of the time we weren't. If you could see the holes in them, you'd understand why we lost so many."

Fewer than four percent of those who received medical attention in the field or were evacuated during World War II died from wounds or disease. In Mary Damon's tent, where the worst cases were sent, seventy-five percent died.

As the planned advance into France bogged down and casualties went up, doctors and nurses worked around the clock trying to save lives. "Oh, we'd stand at those tables sometimes for hours. I have the varicose veins to prove it! It seemed like your mind just worked on your job. You were sort of in a numb suspension. You were on the outside looking in."

As the Germans fought with a vengeance in the hedgerows just beyond the field hospitals, the fighting sometimes came too close for comfort. "We got an order to move back five miles. Well, if we had done that we would have been in the English Channel. So we had to stay put, which meant our artillery was shooting right over our heads. It banged constantly. We were shivering we were so scared. It went on all night long. We were used to the buzz bombs back in England, but being up at the front line was totally different. That was the only time I was scared of death, because we didn't know what we had gotten ourselves into. About six weeks after we were there, I found this big white streak in my hair.

"At times, things got really bad. We had a lot of strafing from the Germans. Some of the doctors would have to get under the tables to save themselves. And I know of a nurse that was killed. She got a piece of shrapnel that hit her in the chest when she was standing in the door of her tent looking up at the sky. She died right away. That was the time for her number to be called. That was the way we lived. We'd say, 'Our number hasn't been called yet.'" Overall, 201 Army nurses would have their "number called" during the war.

Adding to the stress of being near the front, plus the nature of the work, were the living conditions. The nurses and doctors didn't have it as tough as the GI sitting in a foxhole, but it was a far cry from home. Tents, with the ground as the floor (wood plank flooring was usually reserved for high ranking officers), housed four nurses in bunks. Damon's main memory of sleeping in the tent is of the sleeping bags they were issued. "Those were the darndest things. They were terrible! Just like straight jackets, but it's all we had."

As for "the things necessary to be a lady," as Damon puts it, there were none. "We had slit trenches for bathrooms, and I didn't know what it was like to take a bath for six weeks, other than washing up with the water you poured in your helmet. In the winter, they put pot-bellied stoves in our tents, which made it much nicer."

Damon gives a lot of credit to the engineers assigned to her group. "They did a lot of hard work for us and they treated us well. For instance, we didn't have overhead lights in the surgical tents. So the engineers came up with an idea in which they took coffee cans and fixed them up so they could put electric light bulbs inside, and then turned them upside down. They made really nice, bright operating lamps."

From the soldiers' point of view, nurses were angels. They showed the boys tenderness and care at a time when their lives were in the balance. With a gentle touch or a soft word of assurance, nurses were havens from the violence from which they had come. But in Damon's case, she had no time to make that connection. "After our surgeries, we'd have to get ready for the next group of wounded or the next big push, so there was no time to get attached to any of the soldiers."

Two to three field hospitals would work together behind a division. Damon's field hospital followed the 29th Division through August, which meant she followed behind Rocco Russo. Since Russo had an abdominal wound, there's a strong chance he was operated on in Mary Damon's tent.

The field hospitals would hopscotch around each other every ten days or so, depending on the number of wounded. At the end of the ten days all personnel would pitch in to pack up, load everything into jeeps and trucks, then move ahead to where the army had advanced. That was the grind, week in and week out.

But during rare breaks in surgery, doctors and nurses took the opportunity to either sleep or let off some steam. "We had a day of relaxation when we were outside of Carentan. There was this rumor that there was champagne in Carentan. So a driver, one of the main officers, and three of us nurses got in a jeep and went looking for champagne. But a sniper got at us. All three of us in the back got on top of each other, and the driver was driving with just his eyes sticking up above the wheel! We never got our champagne," Damon says with a full belly laugh. "Another group did make it safely and brought us back some champagne that the Germans had left behind."

I asked her if there was any comparison to her unit and the M.A.S.H. unit we've all seen on television. "No. We didn't have time for any of that M.A.S.H. stuff. It wasn't much like that at all. We were just too busy."

By December 1944 Damon's surgical group was sent to Belgium where they found themselves in the opening days of the Battle of the Bulge. Damon was stationed at St. Vith, Belgium, a key road junction that the Germans were ordered to take. One of the American units on the way to meet the German advance stopped at St. Vith to drop off its wounded with Damon's surgical group. The troops then proceeded toward the town of Malmedy, where one of the war's worst atrocities was about to take place.

Overwhelmed by the German forces, those Americans were captured, gathered in a field, then cut down with machine guns. Some 86 of the 140 men were murdered. This has since been known as the Malmedy Massacre and is regarded as one of the worst crimes inflicted upon American soldiers during the war in Europe.

"We were in the Bulge, but we didn't know it at the time." After a few days of fighting, Damon's surgical group was forced to evacuate to Luxembourg until mid-January, when the Americans were able to drive back the Germans.

Damon had crossed the Rhine into Germany by Easter, and by early May was celebrating the war's end in Weimar, Germany. That celebration took a somber tone when her group toured the nearby concentration camp at Buchenwald. There she saw lamp shades made of human skin, room-sized piles of ashes and bones, and survivors who "looked like skeletons dressed in clothes."

"While we were in Germany, we were waiting to either be assigned to go home or to the Pacific. One night we were at one of the officers' clubs in a town I don't remember. A lot of the officers were there with some fraulines, which was against the rules. About six of us nurses were in there, too. All of a sudden, someone rushed in and said, "Eisenhower's coming!" So they pushed the fraulines out the back door and got some of the American girls to dance with them. Eisenhower walks in and three of us are still sitting. He walked up to us and said, 'What are you doing just sitting there? Come on and dance.' I couldn't believe it! So I danced with Gen. Eisenhower."

Mary Damon's other brush with fame came when she had to give actor Mickey Rooney a penicillin shot somewhere back in France. "I was flabbergasted. There was this actor that I used to watch with Judy Garland. I just looked at him for a while and he said, 'Well, go ahead and give it to me.' So I got to give Mickey Rooney a shot."

She was back in the States by the fall of 1945. The G.I. Bill allowed her to go back to college and get her degree. She also worked part-time at a veterans hospital in Pittsburgh. "Then one day I got a letter after the Korean conflict started. They wanted to know if I'd go back in the Army. So I thought

that since there's another war on I might as well. I was just short
my degree and like a fool I wrote them back and said, 'If you make me a captain, I'll go back in the Army.' They sent me back a telegram saying, 'You got
it.' But I should have stayed in school for six more months to get my degree."

Since Damon already had front-line duty, she was given the choice of
going to Korea or Europe. "I decided on Europe because I wanted to finally
see it not from the back of a truck or ambulance." Back at an officers' club one
night in Germany, she found herself dancing not with Dwight Eisenhower,
but with her future husband.

"My husband was in the Pacific and I don't think we ever talked about the
war. We'd bring up a few things and that would be it. The less said, the
better. Actually, very few people talked about it until after about fifty years. I
think it was the trauma of what happened. You start thinking about the fact of
all those around you that didn't make it, but you're still here. You wonder why
and you think there must be a being or something that didn't call your number at that time. I think now, we're finally letting go of a past that was hurt-
ful for so many."

After another two years in Europe, Capt. Mary Damon came home to
simply be a mom to her two children, taking the next twelve years off from
nursing to stay home with the kids. After those twelve years she felt the need,
financially and emotionally, to get back into nursing. She then gave fifteen
years of her life to the Delaware Hospital for the Chronically Ill, a very different line of work from the grind of a field hospital.

Mary Damon moved to Hampton Roads in the mid-1980s. Having sepa-
rated from her husband, she wanted to be closer to her children and grandchildren, already living in the area.

In 2001, she has been retired for more than twenty years. At 87, she's a
model for the saying, "Never slow down, never grow old." She preaches the
importance of staying busy, claiming it's the reason she's still going strong.
Although her days of wearing a nursing uniform are over, the spirit of her
work is still very much alive within her. She continues to volunteer her time
as a home and nursing-home companion to those who simply need a friendly, warm person with whom to talk. She fits that description perfectly.

For Mary Damon, nursing has been a life of duty to country and others.
"You can't give it up. Once you're a nurse, you're always a nurse. No matter
what else you do, it keeps coming back to you. During the war, we did it to
help people. We didn't think about the money. It was just to help people."

1944

2000

Much of the respect accorded to the generation that fought World War II stems from hardships endured before the war even began. The Great Depression took its toll on American society. But it also hardened it, preparing it for the war ahead. Ed Cluney was part of the generation that struggled in the 30s and fought in the 40s.

Cluney is a northerner. He may live in Virginia Beach now, but his Boston accent will forever give away his roots. Those roots started during a time of financial despair for his family, as well as millions of others across the country. As a child and young teenager in Boston, he worked at scraping together pennies, nickels, and dimes to help his mom keep the family fed. "I can remember, as a kid, selling newspapers. I would buy seven papers for ten cents. When I sold those seven papers, I made four cents. I'd also go down to Boston City Hospital, stand out front, and sell the Saturday Evening Post and a host of other magazines. I shined shoes. I also went down to one of the union halls and dusted off their cars, and they'd give me a nickel or a dime. I can also remember going behind grocery stores and picking up boxes they were throwing away and taking them home to use for firewood. Also, there was a wooded area behind our house that backed up to the railroad tracks. I knew when to go out when a train would go by. The man would throw a shovel of coal out, and I'd go around picking up coal so we could use it at home."

By the time the war began, the scraping and clawing, which many had done for themselves for so long, was turned toward the war effort. It is for this period that Cluney's memories begin to take on a different tone. He recalls the Victory Gardens that dotted Boston's landscape during the early forties. They were the gardens Americans were encouraged to plant to ensure an adequate supply of food for the troops abroad and the families at home. He recalls turning in used tubes of toothpaste, old tires, scraps of metal, and even ladies stockings (they were used for parachutes), all to help the boys "over there." He was about to be one of them.

By early 1943 Cluney knew it was only a matter of time before his draft number was called. "I knew I was going to get drafted, so I went down to the Navy. But, I had just had an operation. When you're taking the physical they tell you to bend over and spread your cheeks. Well, when they came to me, they looked down there and said, 'Sorry, you don't count'. See, I had just had an operation for hemorrhoids. So, I joke all the sailors around here (Hampton Roads) that I wasn't a big enough asshole to join the Navy!"

Evidently, the Army wasn't as concerned with Cluney's recent operation and drafted him in April 1943, one month after he turned 18. "When you got drafted, you just wanted to go where you could get out the quickest." But at that time in the war, the Army was trying to get people in the quickest they could. Cluney spent the next thirteen weeks at Camp Croft, South Carolina, for infantry basic training.

Near the end of their three months of training, the troops were sent on maneuvers, which was like their final exam, except out in the field. But right before the rest of the platoon was sent out with their full packs at 4 A.M., Cluney and another man were told to fall out. They were then restricted to the company area with no explanation. In a stroke of good fortune, they were told they were being transferred to Ft. Meade, Maryland, to assist in advanced weapons training. It meant they were given a stripe on their sleeves, bumping them up to private first class. It also meant they would be able to stay in the States for seven more months.

But seven months is all that remained before the inevitable trip across the Atlantic. "When we went over, we were on the Queen Elizabeth, and we weren't in any convoy. That's because the Queen Elizabeth would outrun anything, even the German subs." Cluney says that he never thought about not making it back home, but that didn't mean he wasn't scared.

He was assigned to an MP (military police) platoon. The men would act as MPs when needed, but their primary job would be that of an infantryman. He says that MPs sometimes got a bad rap from the regular GIs, but usually that was only when the GIs were on furlough. "Our job was to see that they didn't get into trouble, not to put them in trouble. I never did have to arrest anyone."

By the time Cluney and his platoon landed in France in July, 1944, the invasion of Europe had been underway for more than a month. Finally, after seventy-five days of costly fighting in the French hedgerow country, the breakout the Allies had worked for finally happened. What had been gridlock for weeks turned into a rout of the German army as it retreated to the German border, unorganized, scared, and greatly weakened.

Thousands of Americans and Germans lay dead in the wake of the German retreat. Approximately 26,000 Americans died, while 240,000 Germans were either dead or wounded. "Some of the towns we came across, like Avranches, there were German bodies all over the place, and they had started to bloat. One of the jerky American GIs took his bayonet and stuck it in one of the bodies, and all that gas came out. And the stink, oh my Lord, the stink."

As Cluney moved through France his primary assignment was with the Third Army, Gen. George Patton's Third Army. As Patton and his forces tore through France, Cluney went through places named Brest, St. Lo, Coutances, Avranches. "France, we didn't like. For one thing, the people. In those days, they were very dirty. Their clothing, their appearance, their body. One of the things we noticed that was so strange was that especially in the farmland, you could tell how well off the farmer was by the pile of manure in his front yard. That meant he had more cattle. The other thing we didn't like were the hedgerows. You didn't know what was on the other side of them."

Cluney also vividly recalls a hospital stay he had in France after an accident. "I looked out the window, and I could see all these French people at this horse-race track. I was thinking, 'What the hell am I doing here fighting this war when those Frogs (nickname Americans gave the French) are watching a horse race?' I was really upset with it. Then the chaplain came around and I said to him, 'Look!', as I pointed out the window. And he said to me, 'Do you know what they're doing back home today? They're playing baseball.' He was saying that life goes on." But a few close calls with German snipers in the months ahead would threaten Cluney's life.

One of those experiences came as Cluney was performing his MP duties with the Red Ball Express, the line of American vehicles racing across France. His orders were to ride along with Patton's tanks and, when needed, direct traffic as the massive columns of armor passed through each town. "I remember I was out there directing traffic one time, and a couple of bullets were flashed at me. The driver of the truck that was going by at that time got out and we knew where the shot came from. We peppered it, and we don't know if I killed him or he killed him, but there was a dead German sniper up there."

After France, Cluney spent the early fall in Belgium and Holland. Much of that time he was assigned to Gen. Troy Middleton at company headquarters in Bastogne, Belgium. "When he would go and prowl through the woods, he would go on a half-track (half tank, half truck), and I would go as his bodyguard in the back of the half-track with a .30 caliber water-cooled machine gun." I asked Cluney if he thought that was a bit dangerous, to have a general "prowling around." He said, "If there was no danger, he wouldn't have needed me there".

Cluney also has a story to tell about Patton. "We were on an outpost in Bastogne, Belgium, and all of a sudden this jeep comes up and we see two stars on the front of it. Gen. Patton. He came over and said, 'How's it going fellas?' He asked us where we were from, and when was the last time we had had a hot meal. For us, it had just been the previous morning. So, he sat there on a tree stump with us and shot the shit with us. After a while, his driver returned with hot food and they drove off."

Other than the encounter with Patton, outposts were not fun, or safe, places to be. Outposts were typically 20 to 50 yards ahead of the frontline foxholes. It's been said that they were "the edge of the known world." "Most times, the ground was your mattress, and your half-shelter was your blanket. You heard a lot of noise out there, like the rattle of a tank. The German tanks were noisier. As long as you didn't see them, you were all right."

Snipers were a different story. One night, Cluney was manning an outpost with another GI. The two men were only a few feet apart, crouched down behind whatever they could find, when suddenly the other man was hit. He died instantly. There was no way to know from where the bullet came. There was no way to radio in to let someone know. There was nothing Cluney could do except sit there quietly and wait to be relieved, with a dead American lying next to him.

The numbness to seeing death all around him never softened the impact for Cluney. "Each one was something. Another American. It didn't make any difference if he was black, white, green, or pink. He was an American. You just thanked the man upstairs it wasn't you."

On that note, Cluney says that his faith in God, and the faith of many other soldiers, helped get them through. "We knew God was looking out for us. And if it was God's time to take you home to heaven, then you were going to a far better place. A place where there's no more fighting." The fighting was about to get much worse.

December 16, 1944 was D-Day for operation Autumn Mist, the German codename for what came to be known as the Battle of the Bulge. It was Hitler's surprise attack to drive the Allies away from the German border and to cut the Allied advance into two fronts. The Germans had mustered eleven divisions and smashed like a whirlwind into the Ardennes region against the four American divisions assigned to protect the heavily forested area. Intelligence reports were poor, so there was no way of knowing the extent of the attack. For over two weeks, the Allies were on the defensive in what has been called the greatest land battle ever fought.

One of the heroic pockets of resistance was in the town of Bastogne, Belgium, where Cluney had previously met Patton. Bastogne was at a key road junction that led to the port town of Antwerp, Belgium, the Germans' main objective. There had been a race between the Germans and the American 101st Airborne Division to see who would get to Bastogne first and hold it. The Americans won, but the Germans had them surrounded. One of those Americans in Bastogne was Ed Cluney.

"That's a time that's easy to remember, because the winter of 1944-1945 was the coldest winter in Europe in 40 years. I've got the toenails to prove it. When your feet freeze, you get nails that are real thick and a growth underneath. And you couldn't dig a foxhole because the ground was frozen. So, we just used anything we could find to hide behind."

In the meantime, the Americans fought desperately to hold off the German advance. Food and ammunition were running low. "That was terrible," says Cluney. "It was noisy as hell with the shells, mortars, and small arms fire coming in. There would be times you would be hiding behind a bush or tree stump or whatever and a German tank would only be at arms-length away. It wasn't by choice, I'll tell you that much. It was mass confusion out there. We weren't sure where our lines ended and theirs started."

That confusion during the first days of the battle is echoed by Phil Russo. A retired circuit court judge from Virginia Beach, and the brother of Rocco Russo, Phil Russo was an infantryman near Tettingen, Germany, during the Battle of the Bulge. Although he says the fighting was heavy, he had no idea he was part of the now-famous battle until he read it in a book years later. "What you have to understand is that when you're on the front line, all you know is what's going on right where you are. We'd have to read *Stars and Stripes* sometimes to find out exactly where we were and who we were shooting at."

Meanwhile, the defenders of Bastogne knew exactly where they were. They were in a German noose. The German commander sent a letter by messenger to the American commander, Gen. McAuliffe. It stated, "From the German Commander to the U.S.A. Commander of the encircled town of Bastogne." It demanded an "honorable surrender to save the encircled U.S.A. troops from total annihilation." McAuliffe's now- famous response was, "Nuts!" When the German messenger asked what "Nuts" meant, he was told by one of McAuliffe's staff , 'It means, 'Go to hell.' Cluney said that when the men got word of the general's defiance it acted as a rallying charge, stiffening their resolve to not surrender.

Fortunately for them, by December 23 C-47s had begun to drop tons of ammunition, food, and medicine into the town. It was one of the best Christmas presents they could have had. By the 26th, one of Patton's armored divisions finally broke through the German lines and linked with the American front lines around Bastogne. Bastogne was saved and so was Cluney.

By mid-January the original Allied front had been restored, yet at a tremendous cost in human lives. The total American casualties, wounded and killed, were 80, 987. German casualties in the battle are estimated from 80,000 to 104,000. Of the American efforts during the Battle of the Bulge, Winston Churchill proclaimed, "This is undoubtedly the greatest American battle, and will, I believe, be regarded as an ever-famous American victory".

During the last five months of the war Cluney stayed in Bastogne, with one unfortunate exception. One afternoon he was shown the murderous horror at the Dachau concentration camp. Stories of Jews being gassed, shot, burned, and tortured had filtered through to the Allies during the last few years of the war, but Cluney said he had no idea what was really going on. So nothing could have prepared him for what he saw. Unlike the rest of his experiences in Europe, he doesn't have much to say about what he saw at Dachau. "There are some things you just try to forget."

Despite what the German army had inflicted upon the Americans, and what the Nazis had done to millions of others, he holds the German people in high regard. Even before the surrender, local townspeople would come out to talk to him, or even offer him coffee. He says there was surprisingly little resentment toward the Americans.

An example is that in the weeks after the surrender he acted primarily as an MP in a few small towns in Germany. The MPs were issued dress coats similar to the one Eisenhower wore. The troops called them "Ike jackets." "None of them fit," says Cluney. "So we took them down to a German tailor and they were glad to do it for free. They weren't bitter at all. And you know, in the thirteen months I was overseas, I was in thirteen different countries, and if had to live somewhere else, I'd live in Germany."

By the time he left Germany in August 1945, Cluney had earned five battle medals, all before his 21st birthday. He had taken part in all five of the major campaigns in Europe: The Battle of Northern France, the Battle of Normandy, the Ardennes Campaign, the Battle for the Rhineland, and the Battle in Central Europe.

Cluney spent the next thirty years in Boston. He married twice and had three children. In the mid-1970s he received a call from his sister in Portsmouth that his stepfather, who had also moved to Portsmouth, was terminally ill. Cluney moved to Portsmouth to be with him, but his stepfather died two weeks later. Cluney stayed in town and he hasn't left since.

Ed Cluney has made Hampton Roads his home by immersing himself in his local Veterans of Foreign Wars Posts. He was post commander of Virginia Beach Post 392 from 1981-82. He also served as district commander during that time. From 1986-87 he was elected to serve as Virginia state commander. That position qualified him for a European cruise that would tour much of the ground Cluney had seen and fought for during the war. Part of that cruise would have taken him back to Dachau. He declined the offer to go.

Fifty-five years after the war he can still rattle off his serial number like it was his middle name: 31353782. He is frequently asked to speak to groups about his service in the war, but tries to shrug off the idea that he's any kind of hero. Instead, he lists people like Sen. Daniel Inyoue of Hawaii, who lost an arm in Italy. Sen. Inyoue's bravery and injuries have been well publicized, but due to his Japanese ancestry, he was not awarded the Congressional Medal of Honor until 2000. Cluney also lists as heroes the members of the All American-Japanese unit, one of the most decorated units in the Army. They fought valiantly for an America that had caged their families and friends in internment camps. And he looks up at the wall in his office and points to his picture of Ted Williams. "And he's a hero. Five years in the service. Think of the records he could have broken."

Eighty-five percent of those who served in WWII were drafted, including Ed Cluney. As he mentions that, the thought of all those Americans who were ordered overseas to sacrifice, fight, and die brings a swell of emotion to his voice and tears to his eyes. He recently spoke to a group of Navy personnel. He told them, "You're in the service now because you want to be. You're my heroes."

1945                                                    2000

Them all volunteers. Drawn by the secrecy and mystique, they willingly climbed inside the tubes of steel that could either conceal them from the enemy or seal them in a watery coffin. Their feats were great. They comprised only two percent of the Navy's personnel, yet sank over fifty percent of the Japanese fleet. But they paid a heavy price. One of every four men died, suffering the highest percentage of death in all branches of the U.S. military. Yet despite the dangers and early failures, the United States Submarine Force in World War II proved to be one of the most gallant and deadliest forces in naval history.

John Reed was born in 1914, right as the first shots of World War I were being fired. He grew up in Pennsylvania, far from the ocean, but was attracted to the Navy by the age of 19. "I tried to get into the Naval Academy, but at that time all of the congressional spots available were filled, so I enlisted." After completing the Navy's basic training at the Great Lakes Training Center, he was assigned, fittingly, to the *U.S.S. Pennsylvania*, a WWI-era battleship.

"I reported on there as a recruit seaman. That's as low as you can start. After I had been on board for about six months, I intended to see if I could try again to get into the Naval Academy through the allotment they gave to the fleet personnel. It just so happened that an individual from my hometown got married, which was forbidden back then, and he had to leave the Academy. I ended up with his appointment.

"At that point, they gave me a choice. Number one, I could get a special discharge from the Navy and go home and study in preparation for the Academy. The other choice was to come here to Norfolk and attend the Naval Academy Preparatory School and then take the examination to get in. If I failed, I'd just have to finish out my enlistment. But it was an excellent school and I feel like if I hadn't come to Norfolk I probably wouldn't have made it in."

Five years after starting at the bottom of the Navy's ranks back in 1933, Reed graduated from the United States Naval Academy as Ensign Reed, and was promptly assigned to a heavy cruiser, the *U.S.S. Northampton*. After two years on board, Reed's plans turned toward the Navy's stepchild: submarines. " It just seemed like a fascinating type of duty. I don't think I ever rationalized why. It was simply an entirely different kind of service, being that it was all volunteer."

The submarine branch of the military was a relative neophyte in the 1930s, having only been around for a little more than thirty years. The Germans used them well during WWI, and would again during WWII, but their actual value and purpose to the United States was still in debate. Most of the higher brass viewed them simply as patrol boats that would help locate enemy ships so the important part of the Navy, the carriers, battleships, and destroyers, could show up and do the fighting. Pearl Harbor would change all of that instantly.

After completing the officers' three-month submariner school in New London, Connecticut (the school was previously six months long, but had been shortened to three as tensions with Japan grew; Reed's class was the first to attend the three-month course), Reed was assigned to one of the Navy's aging S boats, a class of submarines that had been around since shortly after WW I. The S boats are nowadays generously referred to as the "Gallant Ladies." In the late 30s and early 40s they were known as "pig boats." The unflattering name came from their appearance and dismal living conditions. Their instruments, engines, and crew amenities were primitive. The boats had no radar, no sonar, their engines were slow and prone to malfunction, and more importantly to the crew, they had no air conditioning. Due to the heat and clamminess during long dives, the men were typically reduced to wearing skivy shorts, or less. It's a fair assumption to say that the S boats were the mold for "Operation Petticoat."

Although an Academy graduate, Reed boarded S-45, then stationed in Panama, as one of the low men on the pole. "I guess I was 'George,' which means I did any odd tasks since I was at the end of the line. But I was mainly in charge of the confidential publications and communications."

Reed was part of a squadron of six S-boats that had been deployed to Bermuda. While there, they received the shocking news about the sneak attack on Pearl Harbor. "Shortly thereafter, our six S-boats in Bermuda were sent to Panama. We were based on the Atlantic side, but we patrolled on the Pacific side. So every time we went on patrol, we had to transit the canal. The reason they sent us down there is that they were afraid the Japs were going to make a run at the Canal."

The United States had a little more than 100 submarines when the war broke out, 56 of which were in the Pacific, and half of those were ten to twenty years old. There would be more than 200 on duty by the end of the war. With much of the Pacific fleet still smoldering at Pearl, the fledgling, out-of-date submarine force was called upon as a first line of defense against Japanese expansionism. Adm. Chester Nimitz would later state, "It was the submarine force that I looked to carry the load until our great industrial activity could produce the weapons we so sorely needed to carry the war to the enemy. It is to the everlasting honor and glory of our submarine personnel that they never failed us in our days of great peril."

After a short time patrolling the Canal area, Reed's squadron of six S boats, built to stay within fifty miles of shore, were sent out across the breadth of the Pacific to aid in the defense of Australia. "You had to know those S boats to appreciate this, but every once in a while during our trip across, any one of the six would let out a big puff of black smoke, then fall behind the horizon, and we'd all have to wait on her. One sub had to use salad oil on their bearings because they ran out of lubricant. The only thing that kept those boats running were the old timers who knew all their faults. You were fighting the boat so much that the last thing you wanted to see was a Jap ship."

Their first stop past Panama were the Fiji Islands, where the crews received quite a welcome. "The natives put on a little ceremony for us called a Shark Tooth Ceremony. The chief of the tribe would give a shark tooth to the senior officer in our group. They had a drink they called kava. It's made from the peppermint root. It had no effect on you until you tried to get up, and you found you couldn't. I found out later how they made it. The women would chew this peppermint root all day long and spit it into a common bowl, then ferment it. That's kava."

After the kava wore off, the submariners headed to Brisbane, Australia. "We started up the river to Brisbane and as we got closer we noticed there was quite a crowd on the dock. As we looked closer, we noticed they were almost all females, since the male Aussies were over in North Africa fighting the Germans. So, it turned out to be quite an interesting visit. The only way we ever got any rest was to go out on patrol."

And those didn't offer much of a rest either. Patrols were long, often stifling journeys that lasted 45 to 60 days at sea. It was dive and drive. No ports, no layovers, no dropping anchor. Just endless patrolling, chasing, and running. For the standard S-boat crew of 40-plus men packed into a tube about the size of three box cars, privacy was nonexistent, living space at a premium. Some bunks sat atop torpedoes. A film of oil coated the men's clothes early in their two months at sea, not to be completely cleaned until the boat returned to port. Reed comments, "Since it was an all volunteer outfit, any time somebody said they had had enough, they were allowed to transfer. But it was the other way around. People were trying to get on board.

"Whenever we were north of twenty degrees south latitude, we had to stay submerged during the day. Well, that turned out to be about a fourteen-hour dive. It was pretty rough. After a couple of days of that everybody got rid of their mattresses because they got wet and clammy since we had no air conditioning. And after a couple of hours submerged, you couldn't smoke because there wasn't enough oxygen to light the cigarette. And there was very little cooking of food while submerged, since that used up oxygen also. That lack of oxygen starts to get oppressive. When we would surface at night and open the hatch, you'd say, 'What's that foul smell?' It was fresh air."

Reed also remembers with a chuckle that their charts for that part of the Pacific were less than precise. "The best charts we had were the ones we got out of National Geographic!"

The S-45 made three patrols out of Brisbane up toward the Solomon Islands. The squadron's mission was to find and destroy any enemy vessel, but lack of speed and numbers made their effectiveness negligible. Plus, with no radar or sonar, detection of the Japanese ships was difficult. "We had sound gear, but it was very rudimentary. It was made of crystals, and you would listen from the torpedo room using a stethoscope." The S boats did do some good, though, with the sinking of a cruiser and a few merchant ships. Yet even the newer submarines were having a tough go of it in those dark, early days of the war in the Pacific.

One of the biggest obstacles the underwater fleet had to overcome was faulty torpedoes. Time and time again during 1942 and into mid-1943 captains would set their sights dead center on a Japanese vessel, only to either have the torpedo miss the target completely, explode before impact, or even hit the ship as a dud. Frustrations ran high, missed opportunities higher. Not until almost two years after the war started were U.S. submarines sent out with a torpedo that actually worked.

The S-45, and Reed, were sent back to the States by 1943. Later that year, Reed received orders to report to another S-boat, the S-41, in Dutch Harbor, Alaska. This time, it was as the ship's captain. "In those days, you didn't have to wait long to go from being a George to being in command. The promotions came pretty fast."

Reed comments that the division between officers and enlisted on a submarine was a bit of a gray area compared to the surface fleet. "There is a line, but it's accepted and acknowledged. The fact was, we were all volunteers, and

139

you had to depend not only on the commanding officer, but on the lowest guy on board. The commanding officer is important, but I would like to give more emphasis to the crew. Without every man doing his duty in an exemplary manner, it would have been a futile endeavor. It was a very fraternal atmosphere. We were all in it together. "

After a few weeks in the great white north, Reed was ordered to take the S-41 to Pearl Harbor, where the crew performed services in helping train the anti-submarine forces.

Up to this point, Reed had spent all his time inside an outdated S-boat. That changed in late 1944 when he was given the opportunity to serve on his first fleet submarine, the *U.S.S. Seadragon*. The fleet boats were the upgrades the Navy had started producing in the mid-1930s. They were faster, better equipped, and were much deadlier weapons than the S boats. They carried a larger crew of 80, yet were more comfortable. They could stay submerged for up to 72 hours and could travel 10,000 miles without refueling.

Not only was he on a better boat, but he had been ordered to the *Seadragon* as her executive officer, which meant he essentially ran the boat and the crew. He was also the prospective commanding officer, meaning he was there to train to become skipper of his own fleet sub.

While XO for only two patrols, he was part of a crew that put several Japanese Imperial Navy and merchant vessels on the bottom of the Pacific, an accomplishment that would win him the Silver Star.

Submarine crews would often spend hours, even days, tracking either a single Japanese vessel or a convoy. Initial sightings of the enemy would usually come when the submarine was on the surface. A lookout would spot a tinge of smoke on the horizon, or when the submarine was submerged, a sound operator would see a blip on his screen. The enemy's speed and course were then plotted against the submarine's speed and course, from which would come the proper angle of fire that was fed into the torpedoes' controlling gyroscopes.

As the sub closed in on its prey, the boat typically dove to periscope depth, which was approximately sixty feet. As the captain would peer through the periscope he was able to distinguish what type of vessel they were hunting. Updates were relayed to all parts of the boat as the intricacies and dangers of the stealth approach demanded each man's complete attention to detail. As the captain narrowed the gap, setting up in his desired firing position, the commands of "Bearing-Mark!" then "Set!" then "Fire!" would be given. Counting the seconds as the torpedoes raced toward the enemy's steel hull, men waited to hear the gratifying rumble and thud of a direct hit.

Reed says, "If it's a good shot, there's not much they can do. It punches a good size hole, which will either break the keel, or rupture it enough to sink it. You can actually hear the ship breaking up as it's sinking. The twisting metal is a very definite sound."

Such was the scene played out by Reed and the crew on the *Seadragon* in September of 1944. "One night we made contact with a carrier, three cruisers, and several destroyers in the South China Sea. Shortly after firing at the carrier, a destroyer bore down on us, only 1,700 hundred yards away, which forced us to dive in a hurry. I remember that vividly. I was in the conning tower at the time, and people came falling down the hatch because we sounded the diving alarm. We were full out on four engines trying to get out of there."

One of the *Seadragon's* torpedomen described what happened after that. "Almost before the boat was completely submerged we heard the first explosion, then another and another and finally the fourth. We surfaced about three quarters of an hour later but the sea was empty. There was no way of telling whether or not the carrier had sunk or what damage we had done, but it was a thrill to have hit them four times with four fish (torpedoes)." Later intelligence reports did verify that a Japanese aircraft carrier was sunk that night in the area.

Being on a submarine was dangerous business during World War II. When the boat surfaced to recharge it's electric batteries, she was a sitting duck for strafing, bombing aircraft. Enemy destroyers and escort ships hunted them ruthlessly with depth charges. Basically a big can filled with high explosives, depth charges could not only shake a man to the bone, but also could rupture a ship's hull, making it a grave for all hands. Reed says flatly, "In submarines, you never got wounded. You either came back or you didn't. You didn't worry about losing an arm or a leg.

"The first thing you hear from a depth charge is the detonator that sets the charge off. It sounds like somebody hitting the hull with a hammer. Then you get the rumble of the explosion. They said that as long you heard the detonator, you were alright. If it's sufficiently close (50 feet), it can rupture the hull. That could flood a compartment pretty quick. You could seal off that compartment, but you can't lose too many compartments, and one could get you in trouble, depending on where it is.

"We had occasions when the air compressors were knocked off their foundations by depth charges, and early on they'd break all the lights. So they eventually started hanging the lights on wires so that they wiggled instead of broke.

"And there's no such thing as a safe depth to get away from depth charges. But there was one thing that could help you out. What we had mounted in the control room was a bathythermograph. It was basically a thermometer that recorded the temperature of the water as you went down. And what you would hope for during an attack was to get below a discontinuity, which would be a spot where there would be slightly colder water above slightly warmer water. It was an inversion. If you could get in that, when the enemy ships would ping you (using sonar), the signal would just bounce off and then you could get through. All you had to do then was to just sneak away. But if you couldn't find that inversion, you just had to take it."

By early 1945 the United States Submarine Force had cut the lifeblood flowing into Japan. Being an island nation, the Japanese depended on merchant shipping to bring in supplies from their lands of conquest. But month after month, U.S. submarine crews were sending not only Japanese Navy vessels to the bottom, but precious oil tankers as well. By the end of 1942 the subs had claimed only 180 ships. By 1943 that number climbed to 335 for the year. At the end of 1944, submarines had nearly worked themselves out of a job. With finely honed tactics and an array of new equipment, the sub crews had decimated the Japanese merchant fleet, and had sunk almost one third of the Imperial Navy. It was during these death throes of the Japanese fleet that Reed was tapped as Capt. Reed of the highly decorated *U.S.S. Sunfish*.

"I was ordered to the *Sunfish* as commanding officer in March of 1945. Targets were getting pretty slim, so we were starting to do patrols in the Sea of Japan. Well, we were charging batteries one night, and we got an Ultra message (Ultra messages were so sensitive that they were referred to as "burn before reading messages") that let us know there was going to be a Japanese convoy departing from port at 8 A.M. It told us how many ships and escorts. So, we finished up our battery charge and headed up the coast to Hokkaido, to the entrance of the port. As we were heading to the port, there was a Japanese anti-submarine vessel patrolling. I didn't want to do anything to it because I didn't want to reveal that we were in the area. But we did get a torpedo ready, and kept it in his direction. He made a complete patrol around us, went back into port and gave the all clear.

"Well, he then came out leading this convoy, and he was the first one we fired at. He was such a beautiful target that we couldn't let him go. Then we fired at the lead merchant ship, and then at another. We fired six torpedoes at only two ships, but in their confusion the escort was sunk and three merchant ships were sunk. We fired spreads, so the other ships had stepped into the paths of the other torpedoes. I'd rather be lucky than good."

It wasn't yet time to start feeling lucky. As soon as the other vessels were hit, three more Japanese escort ships raced toward Reed's position. What ensued was likely one of the longest days he and his crew ever spent on a submarine. Reed gave the order to dive deep as the *Sunfish* tried to escape. He was lucky to find a two degree temperature inversion that offered some protection from being located by the sonars pinging at him from above. He then had the crew rig for silent running, which meant shutting down any unnecessary machinery that might give away the sub's location.

The crew was in for a pounding. Only one mile off the Japanese coastline, the *Sunfish* was pursued doggedly for much of the day. "We were worked over by three escorts that knew their job well. We counted a total of fifty depth charges. We had to just creep away, because we couldn't outrun them. Then, at 6:55 that evening, we finally surfaced after a grueling sixteen-hour dive." Reed and the crew of the *Sunfish* had endured ten to twelve hours of depth charges that exploded around their boat with no significant damage.

After escaping, the *Sunfish* continued to patrol off the Japanese home islands of Honshu and Hokkaido. Catching two other ships just four miles off the coast of Hokkaido, Reed sank them both, putting the *Sunfish's* bag of ships for just one patrol at six, with a seventh damaged.

"Here's something interesting about the events during that night attack. We were on the surface and we happened to look out on our port side, and here was this streak coming right at us. We thought it was a torpedo. But what is was, was a porpoise that had come up. That was scary."

Capt. Reed's actions during that patrol earned him the coveted Navy Cross, second only to the Navy's Medal of Honor. The entire crew of the *Sunfish* was awarded a Navy Unit Commendation for its actions. "There weren't many ships out there by then, so it's amazing we were able to do that."

That was the eleventh and final patrol of the *U.S.S. Sunfish*. With all her torpedoes spent, she headed back to Pearl Harbor. "We were on our way back, and we heard that they dropped the atomic bomb on Japan. We didn't know what the hell they were, but they sounded pretty good," smiles Reed. "After we got back to Pearl, we started to get ready for the invasion of Japan, but then the war ended. I remember that all hell broke loose on the streets of Honolulu, and I said, 'Hey, I got this far. I'm not going to get killed out there,' so I just went back to the hotel."

As Reed finishes telling his story to me, he comments that it's not something he even thinks about any more. "It's the people that do think about it that have the problems. It can get to you. And it doesn't bother me that a lot of people now don't know what I did, or what others did."

In my opinion, not enough people fully realize what men like John Reed and the other submariners did for our country. In writing one of the greatest chapters in U.S. naval warfare, they sank more than 1,300 enemy ships, helped sever the lifeline of supplies flowing to Japan, scouted and laid minefields, ferried troops and cargo, and rescued downed pilots, including former President George Bush. But in doing the tasks asked of them, 3,505 men from 52 submarines were killed, sent on what their fraternal brothers call "eternal patrol."

The year 2000 was the centennial celebration of the United States Submarine Force. As part of that commemoration, Nauticus Naval Museum in downtown Norfolk displayed the *Sunfish's* battle flag of 42 destroyed Japanese ships. Beside that flag was a sign honoring not only the crew of the *Sunfish*, but the deeds of Capt. John Reed.

# DAVID KATZ

2000

Ihave struggled to write some sort of meaningful, telling introduction to David Katz's story. I cannot. Unlike other chapters in this book, his is not one of heroism, patriotism, or bravery. No, it is simply one of numbing disbelief and sadness. That is the feeling I had after he told me how he survived the Holocaust.

Most of us know at least something about the Holocaust. We've either seen *Schindler's List*, read *Anne Frank's Diary*, or seen something about it on television. But to hear about it from someone who was actually there is a completely different, and powerful, experience. He survived, yet six million of those that shared his Jewish faith did not. They were murdered. Men, women, children.

As you read Katz's story, please remember that on paper they are only words. Try to imagine listening instead of reading. For it is his hope that generations to follow will continue to listen.

"I was born in 1930 in Leipzig, Germany. My parents were both professional musicians, having graduated from the Leipzig Conservatory of Music. Leipzig was more or less the musical capital of Europe. A lot of very famous composers such as Bach, Mendlssohn, Schuman, Wagner, Teleman, all had their homes in Leipzig. I started my musical education early, of course. I studied piano and violin, starting at about three. So that was my beginning.

"But my musical education was interrupted by the Holocaust. Hitler took power in 1933 and from that time on was the beginning of the discrimination against the Jewish population in Germany. At that time, things were very bad in Germany. Unemployment was like 50 to 60 percent. A lot of people didn't have money to buy food. Hitler found an easy scapegoat in the Jews and blamed them for German problems.

"Starting in 1933, a lot of children were killed. German children, non-Jewish children, supposedly because they were retarded. In some instances, some parents would turn their children in for disobedience. Well, the Nazi regime would say that if they're disobedient, they're mentally retarded and those children were taken away and never heard from again. The Nazis did things that were atrocious.

"Also, school children, five or six years old, would eavesdrop on their parents' conversation. If they overheard their parents say anything against the Nazi regime or against the treatment of the Jews, those children would report them to the Gestapo and the parents would be arrested the following day. It was a difficult time. But in general, the Nazis seemed to enjoy inflicting hardships or pain on people and not just Jews.

"Later on in 1935 in the Nuremberg Declaration, the Nazi regime took away all the civil rights from Jews in Germany. We were no longer allowed to vote. We couldn't teach in the universities or public schools. Gentiles were not allowed to deal with Jewish merchants. They couldn't use Jewish doctors. Jewish doctors were only allowed to treat Jews. We didn't have access to entertainment media or movie houses. We couldn't sit on park benches. There were big signs on them that read, 'No Jews, No Dogs.' It was all right for Jews to walk on the sidewalks as long as there were no Aryans in sight; then we had to walk quickly on the street, no matter what the vehicular traffic was like.

"In 1936 I started school but I was not allowed to go to school with the rest of the kids. So there was a rabbi in Hamburg who established schools throughout Germany for the education of the Jewish children. We went to the one in Leipzig. My cousin Wolfgang and I would go to school together and not a day would go by that we would not be accosted by German youths who insulted us with racial slurs and would throw sticks or stones at us.

"At that time, I think it was more frustration than fear. Fear did not come in until later in 1938.

"You have to remember, a lot of German Jews fought on the side of Germany during World War I. They were highly decorated. But it didn't make any difference to Hitler. A Jew was a Jew.

"Many people wanted to leave. As a matter of fact, my parents had just about all the paper work to come to the United States in 1937. We went to Holland with just a few belongings and my father's favorite violin. The Germans did not allow the Jews to remove anything of value from the country, so we were lucky to get at least one of his precious instruments out of Germany. We were supposed to leave for the States from Rotterdam, but there were some glitches with the paper work. While we were waiting there my mother became homesick for her parents. My grandparents still lived in Leipzig. We had all lived in one large apartment together. So we went back to Germany. Big mistake.

"It became increasingly difficult to make a living, no matter what your job or business was. My father worked as a musician until early 1938. He led the orchestra at the Palast Hotel in Leipzig. In those days, the big hotels had orchestras for dancing or for dinner. After our return from Holland, the Nazis would no longer permit my father to return to his post at the hotel. Then he became a shoe repairman. You did anything you had to do to survive. Here was this fine musician with his delicate hands, coming home every night with bloodied fingers that prevented him from playing his beloved instruments. It wasn't easy for Jews in those days.

"Also in 1938, there was Kristallnacht ("night of broken glass"). That began the actual persecution of Jews in Germany. It was the beginning of the Holocaust. That night gangs of Nazis, instigated by Hitler's propaganda machinery, smashed the storefronts of Jewish merchants and looted their stores. It was the end of Jewish businesses. At the same time, all the Jewish synagogues in Germany were set ablaze and burned down. While Jews were trying to make their way back to the safety of their homes, they were brutally beaten and dragged through the streets. That night alone several hundred Jews were killed throughout Germany, and in the ensuing few days thousands more were sent to concentration camps.

"The day after Kristallnacht, the Gestapo, with drawn guns, knocked on our door in the morning. Since my grandparents held Polish passports, they were given one hour to pack a suitcase so they could be taken to the train station to be shipped back to Poland. My parents were also born in Poland, but they moved to Germany during World War I. Because of their young age they didn't have Polish passports. Also, Germany did not consider them citizens, so they became stateless.

"We knew any day the Gestapo would come for us also. It was difficult in those days to get any sort of help because the German population was so indoctrinated against the Jews. They thought of the Jews as some sort of demon. The other thing was the fear factor. If any German was found to be harboring or protecting Jews, their lives were in danger. But my father had a friend, a musician who was a Christian, and he gave us shelter in his home at the risk of his life and that of his family's.

"In December 1938, my father was able to be smuggled out of Germany, and he settled in Brussels, Belgium. My mother and I followed in February. We had to pay a smuggler to lead us across the border and it took the last few cents we had. If we had been caught, we would have been thrown into a concentration camp like so many others. There were a lot of German objectors and critics of the Nazi regime that were thrown into concentration camps beginning in 1933. But after October of 1938, they became extermination camps for the Jews.

"By February of 1939 my mother and I had joined my father in Brussels and we lived there until May 1940. It looked as through we would be able to put our lives back together again, but then Germany invaded France, Belgium, and Holland. We knew it would only be a matter of days before the small country of Belgium would fall, so once again we had to leave.

"My father crossed the border to France and he was arrested immediately and sent to a labor camp in Gurs, a terrible labor camp in southern France. My mother and I went to France by train a few days later, not knowing he had been arrested. After we got off the train in France, the police immediately arrested us, too.

"My mother and I were held in a farm compound surrounded by a tall stone wall topped with embedded broken glass shards. About two weeks after, we were taken by train to the city of Mende to be delivered to the concentration camp Rieucros. It was a camp for women and children. Our first sight of the camp was most traumatic. Row upon row of wooden barracks surrounded by barbed wire fences, with armed guards patrolling the perimeter. Inside the barracks were rows of wooden bunks, two-high, and we slept packed like sardines, with only a straw mattress and a rough horse blanket for bedding. Breakfast consisted of a piece of dark, hard bread and some coffee made from several types of roasted roots. For lunch and dinner, we were given a bowl of soup which was nothing more than some hot water with some cabbage leaves and pieces of rutabaga floating in it. With that kind of food on a daily basis, dysentery ran rampant throughout the camp. It was such a drastic change from freedom.

"I had an aunt and uncle that were able to get out of Germany early in 1939. We were very closely related. They settled in Buffalo, New York. Anyways, they sent us the papers to come to the States, and the fare. Once we received the paperwork to come to the States we were reunited with my father outside of Marseilles , France. The authorities then decided to move us to a camp at Les Milles near the city of Aix en Provence. We were there for several months waiting for our number to come up. The United States, unfortunately, had a very strict immigration quota in those years. Conditions at Les Milles were not much better. It was located in an abandoned brick factory. The humidity was atrocious, and we were constantly sick. We were treated well, however, by the camp commander as well as by the guards. After all, we were about to leave for America, or at least so we thought.

"Our hopes of getting out of Europe came to an end on December 7, 1941 when Pearl Harbor was attacked. Once the United States entered the war with Japan and Germany, we were sent to another camp in early 1942. After three to four months there, orders came from Germany to round everybody up for shipment to the east.

"Everybody thought we would end up in a labor camp. I was barely twelve at that time. But there was an organization in France, the O.S.E., a children's aid society, and they made a deal with the Vichy French government that said children would not be sent at that time. So my parents were taken out of the camp. I watched as they were loaded onto trucks and taken away.

"The children were sent to an orphanage in Limoges in southwestern France. I was in that orphanage for approximately a year. Then rumors started spreading around the orphanage that Hitler had issued orders for the Jewish children in France to also be rounded up, which was a fact as approximately 100,000 Jewish children in France were sent to their deaths.

"So one morning we heard trucks approaching the orphanage and before I even found out what it was, I decided to leave. I remembered my parents talking about Switzerland as being a neutral country and that we would be safe there. So, I decided to go to Switzerland.

"I was thirteen years old, not a dime in my pocket, public transportation was out of the question because what little there was available was mostly just buses, and they were checked. Someone would stop the bus, search it, and ask for identification papers. Of course, I didn't have any since they would all identify me as being Jewish. The trains were used by the military for troop and ammunition transports. There were no airplanes.

"So I walked almost to the Swiss border. It was close to 600 miles. It took about five months. Once in a while I caught a ride with somebody: a farmer's wagon, even a car. I made my way from one town to the next. I slept out in the woods or in a barn. For food, it was whatever I could beg or steal, dig out of the ground or pick out of the trees.

"It was a difficult time because so many French collaborated with the Germans. You never knew who you could trust and who you couldn't. So I never told anyone I was Jewish and I spoke French fluently from when I went to school for a year in Belgium.

"When I got to the Swiss border it was so heavily fortified by the Germans that it was impossible to get across. So, I ended up in the city of Lyon, France near the Swiss and Italian border. It was a very unsafe city. You literally couldn't take twenty steps without somebody asking for identification. The German garrison in Lyon was under the command of a colonel named Klaus Barbie. He was nicknamed the Butcher of Lyon because of the hundreds if not thousands of Jews and Resistance members whose blood was on his hands.

"I stayed in the basement of a house that housed twenty to twenty-five Jews that were hiding. I was only there a month at the most. I decided to go a little farther south and ended up in the city of Grenoble. The same problem existed there. I stayed there for approximately a month, month and a half. While there, I ran into a member of the French Resistance and he told me about a village about twenty miles south of there where a Catholic priest was very helpful to the Resistance. He also helped Jewish people in the area.

"So I went to the village and the first thing I did was contact the priest, and he immediately put me up in his home next to the church. One thing the priest told me will forever stick in my mind: 'The Germans have taken away your parents, your freedom and all you possessed, but the one thing they will never be able to take away from you is your Jewish heritage.'

"The priest put me up for about four months, but the Germans used to come up from Grenoble every week to ten days and do house-to-house searches. They weren't searching so much for Jewish people because there weren't that many Jews in that tiny village. It was mostly for Resistance members.

"After a while, the Germans became suspicious of the priest's clandestine activities, and he could no longer risk hiding me. But he knew of a farmer in the area that needed help, so I went to work on that farm. I befriended the leader of one of the Resistance groups in the area, and from that time on I became a member of the Resistance. I changed my name to Daniel Dupont, and the Resistance was able to provide me with fake documents.

"Whenever the German troops came into the village to do searches, I would join the members of the Resistance in the woods. They would attack the German columns. I was not a part of the attacks because of my young age (14), but they made use of me as a courier. I would deliver messages from one group of Resistance fighters to another, telling them approximate numbers of Germans, whether they had artillery with them or armored vehicles. They were very effective because the Germans never knew who was friendly and who was not. But if any of the French Resistance members were caught they were executed immediately. It happened often.

"I stayed on that farm until the armistice was signed. I was fifteen years old and had seen and suffered enough to last a hundred lifetimes.

"I went to Paris because the American Consulate was there, so it would have been easier to make arrangements to come to the States. After I arrived there I was hoping my parents would still be alive. During the war, very little was known about what was going on in the extermination camps. Everybody thought they were going to a labor camp. But once the Russian troops liberated some of those camps in Poland, the news came out about what went on. And of course, then the Americans and British troops liberated more.

"So in Paris I contacted the International Red Cross in order to find the whereabouts of my parents. It took them about two months to let me know what happened to them. They had been killed in the gas chambers in Auschwitz. My father was 45 and my mother barely 33. My grandparents and the rest of my family were killed in the Warsaw Ghetto in Poland. I did have an aunt that survived Auschwitz. Her daughter also survived by being hidden by nuns in Denmark. I have no way of knowing what happened to the children at the orphanage I was at, but I doubt if any of them survived, except the ones that were able to get away before the Germans came."

By April 1946 David Katz was finally able to leave Europe. He was welcomed into the home of his aunt and uncle in Buffalo, New York. They raised him as one of their own, with his former cousins now his lifelong brothers and sisters. "It was difficult at first. When I came to the States to live with them, they did their best to make me forget."

After graduating high school in half the time expected of him, David Katz moved to New York City to become a furrier apprentice under his Uncle Max. He then later moved back to Buffalo to help his Uncle Leo with his new theater and concession business.

By 1950 America was back at war, this time with Korea. Despite the terror he lived through just six years prior, he received his draft notice in 1951. Ironically, he was not sent to Korea, but to Germany.

"I spoke to hundreds if not thousands of Germans in the two years I was there. Those were the people that committed the atrocities. Not one of them admitted to hating the Jews or having done anything to the Jews. So it was a difficult two years because I just couldn't force myself to have any respect for those people. But today is a different story. You can't hold today's generation responsible for their grandfather's sins."

By the time David had returned home, the family concession business had grown considerably. It continued to diversify and expand, eventually reaching into several northeastern states and Canada. David's own family continued to grow as well, as he and his wife MaryAnne celebrated the birth of four children.

In 1994, at age 65, he retired and moved south to Chesapeake. His business life was behind him, but a new opportunity was presented. In 1996 he was invited to become a member of the Holocaust Commission of the Tidewater Jewish Federation and also a member of their Speakers Bureau. It has served as a chance for David Katz to be a voice for the six million Jews murdered in Europe.

"I started speaking shortly after I arrived here in Tidewater. At first it was difficult to talk about the Holocaust, to live it a second time. But I got used to it. I tell you, when I speak, whether it's to children or adults, the attention and respect that they show me is great. They show a sincere interest in what happened. My main message is to teach tolerance, and it's mainly toward children because it's going to be up to them to grow up without prejudices to prevent holocausts from ever happening again."

1945

2000

"The only reason I'm willing to talk to you about this is I want people to know what we did over there. What we went through. I want younger generations to know something of the sacrifices made by my contemporaries in ending Hitler's dream of Nazi domination. But I'm no hero. I didn't do anything special, and I'm certainly not looking for any glory."

Eddie Cooper was determined from the beginning to set me straight. He knew why I was coming to talk to him and why others have in the past. He shrugs it off by saying, "You really ought to talk to somebody who knows a little more. I was only in combat for five days."

On his fifth and last day in combat, his life, and body, changed forever. It happened as a German shell fragment ripped into his leg. But Cooper says the real story isn't about what was eventually left of his leg. No, he says, the real story, the grim reality, is about how insane war is, and how sad it is that so many American boys didn't come back at all.

He was born at Norfolk Protestant Hospital, now known as Sentara Norfolk General. Immediately after graduating from Maury High School in 1942 at the age of 17, he entered the Wartime Accelerated Program at Virginia Polytechnic Institute as a cadet in the ROTC program. As a "rat," he was assured of completing at least one year of college. Most students never even finished their freshman year, at Virginia Tech or any other college in the country. They were all being drafted. So Eddie knew it was only a matter of time before the draft board called his number. He decided to try to dictate under what terms that would happen.

Being in the Wartime Accelerated Program may have enabled Cooper to complete one year of schooling, but it wasn't enough to qualify him for Officers Candidate School. Two years were needed for that. Therefore, he would be up for grabs in the general draft. In a race to further his schooling before being drafted, he and a number of his friends took the Navy's V-12 exam. It was the Navy's version of allowing qualified young men to go through school on an accelerated basis, later to be assigned to Naval duties. "I waited and waited to hear how I did on the V-12 but I never heard. All of my friends had, though, so I thought I hadn't passed. So, I finally went down to the draft board and said, 'All right, let's hurry this thing up. ' I asked for the Navy or the Army Air Corps, but I got the Army.

"On my first day at Camp Lee in April of '43, my mother was able to contact my company commander to tell him that a letter from the Navy had been delivered to the wrong house about a month and a half ago. Come to find out, I had passed the Navy V-12 exam, and I was supposed to report for the Navy medical the next day!

"In a rare show of sympathy, my company commander arranged a three-day pass for me to return to Norfolk to take the exam. Of the 75 men examined that day, only 16 passed. I was one of them. But all attempts to get transferred into the Navy failed. Once you're in the Army, you're in. There's no transferring out."

Cooper remained at Camp Lee for about three weeks when a telegram was delivered from the Army Adjutant General stating that Cooper was being recommended for the Army's new ASTP program (Army Special Training Program), which was similar to the Navy's V-12 program.

Three months would pass before the recommendation would come to fruition. Those three months were spent at basic training at the Aberdeen Proving Ground in Maryland, where he learned how to repair sensitive instruments such as prisms and other optical instruments for tanks. Finally, Cooper was reassigned for ASTP training, which just happened to be back at Virginia Tech.

"VPI at that time was known as a star unit - one of the collecting points for those who qualified for the program. From there, we were assigned to various colleges all over the country. I stayed at VPI. But after being there for only six months, the program was revamped. With the invasion of Europe on the drawing board, the Army needed to build its ranks of fighting men. They needed people in the field. So all of a sudden we found ourselves being boarded onto troop trains and put into the infantry. Believe me, those trains were full of sad sacks."

As quickly as that, Cooper had gone from the collegiate air of Virginia Tech to being a buck private in the 84th Infantry Division. Some 2,800 other recent ASTP men were in the same predicament. As soon as they arrived for basic training they were told, "You college Joes will now find out what the Army is all about!" Actually, the ASTP men were welcome additions due to their age and collegiate experience. Regardless, what followed was intense, grueling training in the summer heat of Louisiana. "I'll never forget the stinking swamps, the humidity, the mosquitoes, the chiggers, and yes, the snakes. We all thought we were being trained to go to the Pacific. But in early September, 1944, we boarded troop trains for New Jersey to head out for Europe."

As American casualties skyrocketed following the invasion of France, ship after ship of fresh American boys, including Cooper, left the States and headed for Europe. His ship spent ten days making the crossing and landed in Southampton, England, on October 1.

"We were billeted in private homes in Alresford. The people had moved out, and we just took over the houses, which were then furnished with wall to wall tiers of bunks. During the entire month of October, we spent our days marching around the streets and doing calisthenics and simply waiting for our orders.

"I loved England. I met a wonderful family in Alresford on one of our first evenings there. There were four of us that hung out together, and we met Mrs. Hartland and her daughter, Nghare, at a small service club hosted by the Women's Voluntary Service. We started joking around and carrying on with them one night, and we ended up walking them home. They were genuinely nice people and we all just seemed to hit it off. Mrs. Hartland said, 'I like you boys and I'd like you to come and have afternoon tea with us when you're free.' We quickly accepted, and it got to be a habit. We went back a number of times and we tried to show our appreciation by bringing them candy and cigarettes. We even went horseback riding with them and had a great time... for that one month. Mrs. Hartland took the names and addresses of our closest relatives and wrote to each of them after we were shipped out."

On Halloween night, 1944, Cooper's 84th Infantry Division sailed from England to France. Cooper's unit landed on Omaha Beach. "We landed there just like they did on D-Day, but of course there was no combat. There was still a lot of wreckage in the water and on the beach. I thought about what those guys had to go through as I looked up from the beach to the cliffs and German bunkers. I thanked my lucky stars I didn't have to do it."

His time was near, though. They didn't know it yet, but the 84th Infantry Division was headed directly to the front, which by early November was along Germany's Siegfried Line. It was a formidable gauntlet of gun emplacements, pillboxes, trenches, roads, and command centers that ran along much of the Western Front. At the time, it was the most impressive man-made line of defense ever created. It was behind this line that Germany was to make its last stand to protect the Fatherland.

The Allied advance crashed to a halt along the Siegfried Line. Division after division was thrown against the Germans with only slow gains. Losses on both sides were horrific. Correspondent Ernie Pyle described the war during the fall of 1944 as "a flat, black depression without highlights, a revulsion of the mind and an exhaustion of the spirit." It is what lay ahead for Cooper.

To fill the holes left by the dead and wounded, lemming-like lines of fresh troops, like Cooper's 84th Infantry, were rushed into service. "Fresh off the assembly line," the 84th was one of the many divisions that was part of the stream of mass-produced units full of green, yet well-trained men headed straight for the Western Front.

"Everybody had fear. Of course we did. But we hadn't seen anybody die at that point. Certainly not any of our friends. We had a job to do and we wanted to get it over. We did a lot of praying. Everybody thought a lot about mom and pop back home, girlfriends, wives, and children. We all had a picture, or two or three. And we'd talk about those pictures.

"My dad died when I was seven and I was an only child, so my main responsibility was my mother, and I worried about what would happen to her if I didn't get back. That was my main thought. We all just wanted to be back home.

"But we still complained a lot. We had to march nine miles from Omaha Beach to our campsite and I had brand new boots which put blisters on my feet. Then we were going to set up our tents and they said, 'Hey Cooper, you got a detail to do. You gotta help dig latrines.' You can imagine what I said. I think I had helped dig one or two trenches, and started back to put up my tent and they said, 'Hey! You haven't finished yet. You gotta dig latrines for the officers.' And you can imagine what I said again."

Just a few days later, Cooper and the rest of the men were loaded onto trucks for quicker delivery to the front. "We were part of the Red Ball Express and we still didn't know where we were going. Part of our trip took us through Paris. We spent ten minutes there for a lavatory break in a park. It was gorgeous. There were people riding horses in their little derby hats and I thought, 'My God, I thought there was a war over here!' I had seen the devastation in St. Lo from the initial invasion, but Paris wasn't really damaged. For me, it was free sightseeing."

As the 84th Division left the niceties of Paris, one of the coldest Novembers in decades was descending upon Europe and the troops. As the temperatures dropped and cold rains saturated the ground, the men slogged their way by truck through Belgium and Holland, getting closer to the fighting each day. "It was not only a war against the enemy. It was a war against mud and trench foot, and rain and cold. It was just miserable. I can't begin to tell you how miserable it was." One of Cooper's rare comforting memories of his trek across western Europe centers around several days he and his buddies spent in a barn near Mastricht, Holland. One of his lasting memories of that barn is watching a calf being born, which he says was quite an experience for a city boy from Norfolk.

On November 16 they left the coziness of that barn for the teeth of the German defenses. It was to be baptism by fire. "The 84th was being thrown into a major mission in just over two weeks after its arrival in France. New divisions usually were placed in a relatively quiet sector to give them the experience of enemy fire with a minimum of danger. We were an exception to that.

"We were to help take this little town of Geilenkirchen which the German's held. They took us to a certain point, then we had to walk, run, crawl, or crouch the rest of the way. One thing they told us was 'Carry all the food you can take because we don't know how often we can get food to you.' So we stuffed cans and boxes in our shirts and jackets. The first time we were under shell fire we hit the ground, and with all that food we couldn't get close enough to the ground! When you're under fire and you're on the ground, you want to be like a snake and disappear if you can. We were throwing food every which way to get rid of it! If we got hit, we wouldn't need that food anyhow. A couple of guys were killed by shell fire on the way up.

"One of my friends yelled to me when we were throwing food out, 'Coop, I'm not going to make it! Call my wife and tell her I love her!' I said, 'Oh, come on, it's OK!' He was OK then, but he was later killed. He was from Chicago. I never found his wife."

On their last night before reaching the front line, Cooper's unit stayed in deserted German homes in a small village. "Whatever soldiers had stayed there before had desecrated it. They had taken the cupboards down and smashed them. But war is like that. You see your people hurt and killed and you want to hurt others. It sort of bothered me, though, and I don't think I would have done that. And I remember that upstairs there was a marriage license and pictures of that German couple. It gave me a lot of mixed feelings. What happened to these folks? Were they part of the Nazis? Where did they go?"

"Also, on our way up to the front the next day, we passed a line of German prisoners that were on the other side of the road. They were laughing, talking, and asking for cigarettes. We looked at those fellas and thought, 'Hey, they look just like us, and we're going up there to kill them. And they're trying to kill us. This is insane.' War doesn't make sense. It's hard to accept. Of course, we knew it was either kill or be killed."

Despite the throngs of Germans that were surrendering, thousands of new German soldiers were being piled into the Siegfried Line. They may not have been the finest German soldiers, but they were capable enough to fire a machine gun or launch a mortar. Dug in behind walls of concrete, wood, and mud, with guns crisscrossing the countryside, they waited for the Allies, including Cooper, to advance.

"As we moved up to the front under nightfall, you really couldn't see where you were. You could see fires in the background, and I remember flares being shot in the air. They'd have us under shell fire for a little while, then we'd move up a little farther. Then more shell fire. Then move a little farther. We were just sort of like sheep. You go along where they tell you to."

Most of the men, including the officers, had never been in combat before. Months of training did little to prepare them for what they were up against. Machine guns, mortars, and heavy artillery shells rained down.

During the night, they slowly worked their way across an open, muddy field dotted with shell holes as they closed in on their front-line stand. With few places to hide, the men stopped to furiously dig foxholes. Cooper had lost his shovel, so he had to dig with his bayonet, and even his hands while his foxhole buddy worked with his shovel. "When daylight came, we were shocked to find ourselves way up in front of everybody in our double foxhole. I don't know how we got up there."

Five days later, the sun was setting on November 23. As soon as darkness fell, the men were told to move out. It was a night that would change Eddie Cooper forever. "I remember we had jumped in some trenches. They might have been German trenches, I don't know. I think there were some bodies in there. Then we jumped out and moved up, and had to hit the ground as artillery and mortar fire seemed to have us zeroed in. We couldn't move forward until the shells stopped coming in. All of a sudden I thought a rock hit me in my thigh. It didn't even hurt. Then I felt something really warm running under my leg. I started to get up and ooh! The femoral artery in my upper thigh had been severed by a shell fragment about the size of the end of your thumb.

"I was losing blood fast. I yelled, 'My leg! My leg!' Then I went into shock. It was wet, cold, I was shaking. I remember somebody picking me up, by my legs, and tossing me in a foxhole. Someone had to have put a tourniquet on my thigh. If not, I would never have survived. I've always wondered who saved my life.

"I remember shaking all over, and they put a wet raincoat over me because that's all they had. It's all really vague, but I do remember the pain and the cold. Next thing I remember, they put me on a stretcher and loaded me on a jeep. One of our sergeants, Sgt. Montleon, was also on a stretcher beside me. Ended up he didn't make it. I was in and out, so I only remember bits and pieces. But I vaguely remember being on the jeep."

Cooper remembers nothing after that. The account of what happened next comes from a letter he received several months later. One of his good friends, who was there that November day, wrote to him, detailing the near-death trauma. Cooper discovered he was rushed to a battalion aid station for emergency treatment. Although the medics were able to stop the bleeding, Cooper had lost so much blood that he was given up for dead. Thinking death was imminent, the chaplain on duty had taken Cooper's personal belongings, as is customary, to forward home. But Cooper clung to life. Miraculously, his body rallied after being fortified with more plasma. Strengthened slightly, he was forwarded to a hospital.

"When I came to I was in a basement of a monastery. There were guys on stretchers all over it. From there they put me in a hospital ward with guys that were really bad off. I mean bad off. A number of them expired. The doctor came in every day for nine days and stuck pins in my leg. As he'd go down, I'd say, 'Ow! Ow! Ow!' Where I didn't say Ow! they'd make a little mark." Cooper says he tried not to think about what that mark meant.

"By early December they told me what they were going to have to do. All I could think about was, 'What am I going to do at the beach?' I loved Virginia Beach and the surf."

The mark on his leg was just above his ankle. It's where the blood had stopped circulating and gangrene had set in. That's where the doctors cut. After the amputation, he was taken to an airplane hangar in Leige, Belgium, for transport to England, but bad weather delayed his needed delivery to a larger hospital for two days. That delay meant penicillin supplies were stretched thin. Unable to receive the amount of infection fighting medicine he needed, Cooper's leg again became infected with gangrene. "I was really sick. My fever went way up. By the time I got to England I was delirious, so they tell me. Things were really bad. They put me in a private room, and they don't put you in a private room unless they think you're going to die. The chaplain came in. I could get out a word or two, but I just couldn't talk. Somehow I got through to him that I was from Norfolk, and he knew my minister. I believe that chaplain was from Lynchburg."

Cooper spent the next few months in England at an Army hospital making a slow, and what sounds like a painful, recovery. He says he doesn't even remember Christmas that winter. Even so, he was soon comforted by dear friends. "When I realized the hospital was less than an hour from Alresford, I had the Red Cross try to contact the family I had become so close to before we left England. They came to visit me just like I was their family. I was able to get a two-day pass to go back with them to their house. They were wonderful, wonderful people. I still keep in touch with the daughter and her husband. In fact, we talk on the phone monthly and they have visited with us here and we have visited with them in England."

By March of 1945, with the end of the war in Europe only three months away, Eddie Cooper was back in the United States. But his home in Norfolk would have to wait. He was sent to another hospital in Atlantic City, where more operations followed. Cooper has several pictures of his time there. They are filled with macabre images of young men, smiles on their faces, yet missing legs and arms. It's sobering to see the numbers of otherwise healthy, young men who looked resilient in their visage, yet were nonetheless hobbled for the rest of their lives by war. It breaks one's heart.

He finally left there with only three inches remaining below his knee. For more than fifty-five years, he has worn a prosthesis.

"There was the vanity concern. You worry about other people's reactions. I worried about the beach, but I didn't stop going. But it has always sort of bothered me. Yes, it does bother me. We all want to be normal and look good. But now, putting my leg on is an automatic thing. It's just put it on and get going."

And "get going" is what he and his wife do all the time. It was over two months before I could finally meet with him due to his packed travel agenda. If ever there's an example of a handicap not slowing someone down, physically or mentally, Eddie Cooper is it.

But his memories, more than his leg, seem to haunt him much more nowadays. As we talked in his Virginia Beach home, pictures of Cooper and those with whom he served were laid on the dining room table. Glancing over the pictures, he points to those who didn't make it back home. With tears in his eyes and a lump in his throat, he says, "He died, and he died, I believe this fellow survived the war, as did this one, and this man also died." Three of the five killed. It was the same story with another group picture.

In Cooper's roster of the 84th Infantry Division, he has put forty-two Xs by the names of those who died in his unit, Company L. That's forty-two men in just one company. Multiply that by the hundreds of companies that fought in Europe and the Pacific and you begin to understand how more than 400,000 American lives were lost during the war.

"It just makes me thankful. I don't know why them and not me. I don't know. It's disturbing. It's very personal. I count my blessings every day and always silently grieve when I allow myself to think about my buddies and all of those guys who made the supreme sacrifice and didn't come home. I'm sure all front-line survivors have asked themselves, 'Why them? Why not me?'"

# HOMETOWN HEROES

William F. "Bill" Moore was an engineer on board C-47s that flew over the "hump" of the Himalayan Mountains into China. George Hughes was a gunner in a B-29 bomber that also flew over the "hump" for bombing missions against the Japanese in China, Manchuria, and Japan. Arnold Linblad and Jim Rodriguez both landed on the Normandy beaches on June 6, 1944. John Roger fought on both the Atlantic and Pacific, serving on an LST and a converted fishing trawler. Robert Brunner is a survivor of the attack on Pearl Harbor. William Frueh helped commission the *Yorktown*, sunk at the Battle of Midway. H.R. "Swede" Hansen was on board the *Wasp* when she was struck by a Japanese torpedo that sent her to the bottom of the Pacific Ocean. W.P. Hogge was an infantryman who earned four battle stars as he fought his way across France, Belgium, and finally Germany.

The common thread of these men, these victorious veterans of World War II, is that they are all residents of Hampton Roads. They are members of our churches, leaders in our community, neighbors to us all. They are the mold for well-worn platitudes that espouse the virtues of democracy in it's fight against fascism. Within them still reside echoes of a critical time in our nation's and our world's history.

Whether for the generation that fought World War II, or any of the other brave generations of Americans who have risked their lives in service to our country, take time to hear their stories. Don't relegate them to the distant past. For another common thread is this: Our today is rooted in their yesterdays.

That lineage surrounds us in Hampton Roads. I encourage you to take advantage of the history lessons our area offers. If not through the people themselves, then through the memorials and museums that grace our community.

David Parker
Virginia Beach, Virginia
2001

# BIBLIOGRAPHY
# BOOKS

*Citizen Soldier, The U.S. Army from the Normandy Beaches to the Bulge to the Surrender of Germany June 7 1944-May 7, 1945* by Stephen E. Ambrose, Simon and Schuster 1997

*The Fleet the Gods Forgot*; The U.S. Asiatic Fleet in World War II by W.G. Winslow, Naval Institute Press, Annapolis, Maryland 1982

*Another Six Hundred* by J. Daniel Mullin 1984

*Up Front* by Bill Mauldin, Norton Press 1995

*Surviving the Day; An American POW in Japan* by Frank J. Grady and Rebecca Dickson, Naval Institute Press, Annapolis, Maryland 1997

*What They Didn't Teach You About World War Two* by Mike Wright, Presidio Press, Novato, CA 1998

*The Old Breed; A History of The First Marine Division in World War II* by George McMillan, Infantry Journal Press 1949

*The Fourth Marine Division in World War II* Edited by Carl W. Proehl, Infantry Journal Press 1946

*War Under The Pacific*, Keith Wheeler, Time-Life Books 1980

*The 84th Infantry Division in The Battle of Germany*, November 1944-May 1945 by Lt. Theodore Draper, The Viking Press New York 1956

*Liberators, Fighting on Two Fronts in World War II* by Lou Potter with William Miles and Nina Rosenblum, Harcourt Brace Jovanovich 1992

# Other Media

U.S. Army Center of Military History

United States Army Military History

Anzio Beachhead Veterans of World War Two

Journal of Allen L. Laurence, www.virtualtexan.com

*The Blast*

www.navyfrogmen.com

United States Marine Corps History

The History Place

Guadalcanal Online

*Patrol*, Magazine of the Pacific Submarine Force, January 2000.

*The Virginian Pilot* Sunday Oct. 19, 1997

WAVES National website

*Foundation* Vol. 17 #1 Spring 1996 Naval Aviation Museum Foundation, Inc.

National Geographic Society, *Battle of Midway*